[redacted]

The Return of Radio Free Bubba

The Return of Radio Free Bubba

Meg Barnhouse • Kim Taylor • Pat Jobe

20 HUB CITY writers project 05

Bubbas, Bubbas, and more Bubbas

©2005 Meg Barnhouse, Pat Jobe, Kim Taylor

All rights reserved. No part of this book may be reproduced in any form or by any electronic or mechanical means including information storage and retrieval systems without permission in writing from the publisher, except by a reviewer, who may quote brief passages in a review.

ISBN 1-891885-41-3
First printing, May 2005

Hub City editor, Betsy Teter
Proofreaders, Beth Ely, Pamela Ivey, Jill McBurney, Christina Smith
Cover photography and book design, Mark Olencki
Title page photography, Carroll Foster
Coffee and Coke®, The Skillet, Spartanburg, South Carolina
50's Streamliner Radio found and won on Ebay® for $17.00, Betsy Teter

Library of Congress Cataloging-in-Publication Data

Barnhouse, Meg.
The return of Radio Free Bubba / by Meg Barnhouse, Pat Jobe, and Kim Taylor.
p. cm.
ISBN 1-891885-41-3 (pbk. : alk. paper)
I. Jobe, Pat. II. Taylor, Kim, 1954- III. Hub City Writers Project. IV. Title.
AC8.B4323 2005
081—dc22

2005003377

Hub City Writers Project
Post Office Box 8421
Spartanburg, South Carolina 29305
(864) 577-9349 • fax (864) 577-0188 • www.hubcity.org

PLAYLIST

Second Time Around

Pat Jobe

As the second Radio Free Bubba collection goes to press, I again question just what it is that we are doing.

Certainly, we hope to entertain. Making people laugh ranks way up there in my list of favorite things. Julie Andrews can sing 'til she's blue about snowflakes that stay on her nose and eyelashes, but give me the laughter of a throng.

No one can question that Reverend Barnhouse and I love attention. Ms. Taylor would sometimes rather split wood than get up on stage, but we've dragged her into enough spotlights that she may be growing accustomed to the gawks of onlookers.

The record needs to show that the November 1998 publication of *The Best of Radio Free Bubba* by the Hub City Writers Project launched the three of us into many a bookstore, church basement, concert hall, and the occasional bar. I even did a couple of shows in a beauty salon called "He and Me," over in downtown Greenville.

Radio Free Bubba signed on October 18, 1989, and for you history buffs, there can be little downplaying the way the world was changing in those heady days. The Berlin Wall fell. Symbolically it fell all over Europe and to a lesser degree in Asia, especially in the Philippines. Autumn 1989 felt briefly like the birth of freedom for people who had never heard of it.

So much of the optimism of those days has dried and flaked and blown away.

But as I allude to in a number of the pieces in this book, the dreams die hard, at least for me. My wiser and more level-headed partners have often joined the chorus of folks who tell me things aren't getting much better and aren't likely to.

But these two wonderful women, Kim Taylor and Meg Barnhouse, continue to be among the best evidence I have that the world is getting better. I like their stories because so many of them have happy endings, and aren't those our favorite kind?

Years ago three friends of mine sat in traffic behind a little girl standing with her arm around her daddy in the front seat of a pickup truck. One of them said, "That's sweet." Another said, "Yeah, but it's dangerous." The third said, "Well, life's gonna be dangerous. It may as well be sweet."

I think Radio Free Bubba, at least for me, is like that.

The Workout Video

Meg Barnhouse

It is 7:35 a.m., and I am collapsed in a chair watching my new kickboxing workout video. Dripping with sweat and gasping for breath, I am remembering the endurance, balance, and coordination I used to have when I was training in karate, back when getting enough exercise was no problem.

Karate ended gradually for me. I injured my arm and had to sit out of class for a while. I fought my way back into shape, but six months later, I jammed my thumb. I sat out for a while, went back and three months later twisted my knee. Maybe, I thought, this is God's way of telling me to find another way to exercise.

I quit karate and thought about what other kinds of exercise I might enjoy. I thought for three months, but I wasn't getting into shape thinking about all the exercises I could be doing. I tried to swim laps. That was okay—for the one time I did it. I used to swim laps three times a week, before I became a karate addict. After karate, swimming felt dull. There is no screaming involved in swimming, no punching, no impact. Swimming laps no longer satisfied my soul.

I thought for a few more months about what kind of exercise I would enjoy. Walking the dog is pretty good exercise, so I started walking the dog. Unless it's too hot. There is a little low-level screaming involved in walking the dog. I might yell when she wraps the leash around my legs. I yell a little when she poops on a fussy neighbor's manicured lawn. There is no punching or kicking involved in walking the dog, not the way I do it. I was definitely missing the punching and kicking. Walking the dog is okay, but I live in the South, so it's been too hot for four months now. My soul is agitated. I feel myself getting crabbier. I need to sweat and pant and turn red in the face.

Two weeks ago I bought a kickboxing exercise video by Stephanie Steele (the name her mama gave her? I think not). Sadly, just buying the thing did not give me back my muscle tone. I walked past the video sitting on the shelf by the TV, but seeing the tape on the shelf did nothing for my wind or endurance. This morning I woke up early. Today was the day! I unwrapped the cellophane from the video and plugged it in.

It was fabulous to be kicking and punching again! It was great to be stretching. I lasted through maybe ten minutes of the workout. As I said at the beginning, I'm dripping with sweat now and writing while the indomitable Stephanie Steele jabs and kicks on my screen. Her tummy is SO FLAT! It looks almost unnatural. Watch how she smiles while she works out, not even breathing hard. I want to be just like that. Maybe I'll eat some oatmeal for breakfast while I watch her. After breakfast I keep her in the corner of my eye while I wash the dishes. I am looking up the number of my karate school in the phone book. I have got to get back there. I'm obviously not going to do this by myself. I need a class. I don't have time for a class. The line is busy. Maybe I will call later. Oh, good, Stephanie Steele is finished. I feel the burn. Maybe it's the oatmeal.

Shooting Stars

Kim Taylor

On November 17, before I went to bed, I got out my down sleeping bag and fluffed it, pulled the foam pad from under my bed, and laid out my sweat pants, sweatshirt and toboggan. I set my alarm for 5 a.m. This was my preparation for the Leonid Meteor Shower.

It was slightly overcast Saturday night. When the alarm went off Sunday morning, I opened my bedroom window to see a star-filled sky. Within two minutes, I was lying on my back in my sleeping bag on the sidewalk in front of my house.

I have tried to watch meteor showers several times in the past, sometimes seeing only one or two streaks of light, sometimes a few more.

But on this night, there was a grand show. No more than a minute passed without a shooting star.

I tried to scan the sky. I could see the meteors

streaking by here and there. Sometimes one after another. Sometimes larger ones that left a trail in the sky.

I laid there smiling for half an hour.

Cars began driving by. I laughed, wondering what the drivers must think if they saw me in a bundle on my sidewalk. I thought of my children at their other home in Montford Cove. I knew they were probably lying on the trampoline staring up into the same sky. We have done this before. Once at the beach with friends, we bundled up on a blanket. The sand was hard; the meteors were few and far between. But it was the adventure I hope they remember.

I thought of the adults I'd known as a child, and could think of no one who would have been outside alone at 5 a.m. to watch shooting stars. My children can name a dozen people who would do just that.

When my nose got numb, I decided it was time to go back inside. I draped the damp sleeping bag over a chair, pulled off the sweats and climbed into my electrically-heated bed.

Remarkably, I was able to fall back to sleep.

It must have been the stardust in my eyes.

Abraham Jesus Frog

Pat Jobe

I believe in planetary transformation. Here's how it'll happen. One day everybody will wake up and say, "Okay, I feel better. Now, let's heal the planet." We will wake up and say it in our own words, but that's what we'll mean. It will take time. Maybe six months, maybe two years, maybe longer, but rich people will give away billions of dollars, and poor people will have plenty of food, shelter, health care, and schools. War will end, and there will be more celebrations, dances, worship services. People who used to not like each other will dance together in the streets. Yes, I believe this. No. I am not a wild-eyed idealist.

I have believed it for thirty years, and have been mystified that people refuse to make it happen. But a fight with my wife shows why it is taking so long. My wife and I don't really fight. I sputter. Her feelings hurt. I suffer and ache as she pulls away and leaves me in the rain while her feelings hurt. I sputtered at 5:22 in the morning. She asked me to take the frog to the vet. You would think any red-blooded, American man would be entitled to sputter at 5:22 in the morning, talking about taking a frog, which I hit with the lawn mower, to the vet.

I sputtered, "Oh, my God," because the spirit of my father showed up, and the spirits of other men I know who don't like frogs or dogs or cats. They laughed at me for spending money on a frog. I hate being laughed at, especially by the spirits of men at 5:22 in the morning.

So there's the problem. That's why we can't have planetary transformation yet. We have to first have the Yes-Baby-I-will-take-the-frog-I-hit-with-the-lawn-mower-to-the-vet transformation. We have to creep to the bathroom where her face is a mask of hurt and confusion, and we have to share about how much she loves dogs and cats and rabbits and deer and frogs and even the moths that she tried to feed to the frog as he lay mangled in his shoebox with holes punched so he could breathe.

The receptionist said this was her first intake for a frog. She asked his name. I said, "Jesus Abraham," and with a perfectly straight face, she asked if we call him "Jesus" or "Abraham." I told her "Jesus." He's out there now, along with stray dogs and abandoned kittens. He lives near the creek behind our neighbor's house.

I was amazed that two veterinarians would spend as much time as they did on Jesus Abraham Frog and not laugh in my face. Dr. Nancy Houston, the first vet who worked on little mangled Jesus, was walking on crutches herself. What a lovely thing, a woman holding a tiny frog in a shoebox in one hand and supporting her own injured leg with a crutch. Dr. Fred Hill explained, yes, indeed the leg would have to come off to avoid infection and to give little Jesus

Abraham a chance of survival. They would clean the other wounds, and, yes, he did have one good eye left. The $25 was a minimum charge, and the rest of you who use Companion Animal Clinic on Blackstock Road in Spartanburg, South Carolina, should not expect surgery on your frogs at that price … unless you name them Jesus Abraham. That may have some influence.

And I would not have hit the frog with the lawn mower if my soul had not been foaming with anger at my fourteen-year-old daughter, who basically showed so much disrespect to my wife that I wanted a well-oiled machine gun. I know, all fourteen-year-olds act that way, and I acted that way when I was fourteen years old, but certainly not in my parents' faces. How can the planet be transformed if peace-loving, old hippies like me can't avoid images of well-oiled machine guns when our fourteen-year-old daughters act the way they all do? But I still believe it's gonna happen anyway. I still believe a day is coming, sweet Bubbas. Ya'll stay tuned to this radio station.

Bug Zapper

Meg Barnhouse

That party at Boyd's place was a clarifying moment for me. I had been in the South, counting the three years spent here as a child and my four years of college, for about the same amount of time I'd spent in the North. I was thinking of myself as assimilated.

Boyd is a good ol' boy. He hunts and fishes. He can find arrowheads anywhere he walks, he just has the eye for them. If the nuclear holocaust comes and I'm still living, I'm going to find Boyd, because he will know what to do.

At this party, we were eating oysters and chicken Boyd had grilled on the grill he made from an underwater mine he found washed up on Sullivan's Island, down near Charleston. It is a huge black ball that he cut in half. He welded pipes in there to run propane to the coals, and it works great. On the highway, when he was towing the thing back to Spartanburg, he said, people who recognized what it was gave his old station wagon wide berth. He was pretty sure it wasn't going to explode, but when he got it home he found the serial number and called the Navy to make sure it was decommissioned. I'm not completely sure that's the truest of stories, but who knows with Boyd? It didn't explode, anyway, and now it's a grill.

Night was falling. Supper was winding down.

Conversation was flowing in a desultory manner, the way it does when you're sitting around in the South with friends and no one's mad and no one's related. I noticed people pulling lawn chairs over to the shed. "Watch this, Meg," said one of my friends. Boyd took the bug zapper from its hook in the shed and put it down on the dirt floor. We sat in a circle around it. It buzzed often, frying bugs. A murmur rose from the crowd. A line of toads formed, coming out from under the workbench, circling around the bug zapper. Six or eight big toads hopped in a circle around the bug zapper, eating the fried bugs, having their own barbeque. I was fascinated—with the toads, with this group of chemists and artists, of schoolteachers and ministers and mechanics, of asbestos removal experts and dancers and college administrators watching the toads, and with my uppermost thought, which was: I went to Duke and Princeton. I am being entertained by toads dancing around a bug zapper. If they could see me now.

Then: Let them see me and snicker. It does not do to get so sophisticated that you narrow the range of things you can find enjoyable. Expand, expand, until at the end of your life you can think almost everything is wonderful. What a wonderful life that will be.

Embarrassed

Kim Taylor

I'm embarrassed. I could actually get away with this one. No one really knows what I did. But, of course, I'm about to confess.

I was in a business office. There were two women "up front." One was younger and conservatively dressed. The other was—eek—probably around my age or older, and while she had on a suit, it was not conservative. She had REALLY big hair, gold chains, lots of rings, and she was chomping gum.

Now that I recall the suit, I realize it was a simple, double-breasted gray suit with a really short skirt. She was wearing a jacket without a blouse. She was tugging at the skirt, pulling the jacket lapels together, chewing gum and running a computer.

This alone should have told me she could handle anything. I saw her talk to the woman she was waiting on and the repair guy who didn't mind interrupting. At the same time, she was helping the other employee.

During all this, she turned to me and asked if she could help me.

Now, here is the embarrassing part: I did not think she would be able to help me. She had this look. This "floozy" look. And in spite of everything I saw her capably handling, I couldn't get over the "look." But since the younger woman could barely handle the one thing she was doing, I said yes and held up the product. The floozy winked at me and waved me over.

She took care of my little problem while answering yet another question from the repair guy, waiting for the computer to catch up with her, and assisting the other woman she'd been waiting on.

While taking care of the three of us, she also arranged lunch times for two other employees and flirted with a third customer.

She never stopped chomping gum. Never let too much cleavage show. And never let her skirt get past mid-thigh.

I walked out of the office in less than five minutes with my problem solved. She was polite and friendly and seemed to be having a really good time handling several dozen things at once.

And I'm embarrassed because I would never have given her credit for being able to find the restroom.

I know all about the book-by-the cover thing.

Yet there I stood in shorts and a t-shirt, badly in need of a haircut, passing judgment on a woman who spends more time in one morning getting ready to go out than I do in two weeks.

This is one lesson that keeps hitting me in the head over and over and over again. I just cannot seem to hold on to the fact that things are not always as they appear. That competence is shown in action, not in wardrobe. And that beautiful people can be really dumb. I can't seem to remember that unattractive people can be brilliant and funny and sweet. And that sexy people can be cruel and shallow. And all of that can be reversed.

My youngest child keeps talking to strangers. I keep telling her not to. She keeps telling me that they looked like nice people.

I keep telling her you can't tell someone is nice just by looking at them. She does not keep this information in her head any better than I do. And that, of course, scares me more than anything.

Hey, I think my fear just canceled out my embarrassment.

Yippee.

Making Frequent Stops

Pat Jobe

Traveling I-85 around Greenville, South Carolina, can be a nightmare made large. It is, like my experience of driving from Long Island into Manhattan as a teenager, the driving equivalent of riding a roller coaster that suddenly loses its way. It is thousands and thousands of people trying to drive closer and closer to each other at higher and higher rates of speed.

Into the midst of this mechanical madness came a sight that truly lifted my heart. Across the back of a white pickup emblazoned in huge orange letters was,

"This vehicle makes frequent stops."

I had to laugh. Make one now, oh little white pickup truck. Stop now instead of bouncing along in the center lane making seventy-five or eighty miles per hour like the rest of us desperate, caffeine-stressed creatures of the six-lane, motorized-buggy bungee jump.

Make one of your frequent stops in front of that eighteen-wheeler who will pitch you into my lane, and we can all play squalling tires, crashing steel, and exploding glass. Let's mash ourselves into that wreckage just long enough to surround the whole mess with blinking lights, fire trucks, and ambulances. Let's all walk away. Oh, what the heck? Let's imagine the whole thing and laugh and go on.

A few hours later on the two-lane blacktop between Honea Path and U.S. 25, I saw another of those white pickups. And son of a gun, guess what it was doing? It was making a frequent stop. Near a meandering creek, just over a bridge, in the driveway of a brick ranch with nobody home, it was making a frequent stop.

I gaped at the contrast. Is a planet of six billion people so clogged that we can't all spend our lives on two-lane blacktops making frequent stops?

I've been to India, a nation a little larger than Texas with four times as many people as our entire population, yet somehow they have found a way to preserve open land, a slower pace, a road less traveled.

Oh, give me a home, where the buffalo roam, and the little white trucks not only make frequent stops, they model that behavior for the rest of us.

About Pat Jobe

Meg Barnhouse

My friend, Bubba Pat Jobe, has a Masters in People Appreciation. He knows how to make you feel smart and good-looking and funny. He makes you think you are the best company in the world, that you are *with* the best company in the world, and anybody in the world would be lucky to be with the two of you. Even when Pat is maddening, you still feel like you'd rather be right there feeling like throttling him than be anyplace else. That's a gift, as far as I'm concerned.

If you are a friend of Pat's, you come home to messages like this on your answering machine: "Hello, this is Benito Jimenez from the International Peace and Freedom Network. You have been chosen as being wonderful today, because our computers have searched and found your face to be filled with light, your mouth to be filled with wisdom, and your heart to be filled with love. Please stand close to your machine, as it is about to become a powerful transmitter that will shower you with waves of peace and freedom. 4 … 3 … 2 … 1 … Okay. Goodbye, and we love you."

If you have a party, you have to have Pat there. Ask him to bring his guitar, and he will play songs he made up about his father, his wife, his neighbors, and you. At my house, late one night, after Wanda Lu Greene sang "A Long Goodbye," one of my favorite songs in the world, she played the guitar while Pat sang a rendition of "Folsom Prison Blues" that had us rolling on the floor. After a brief argument about singing a John Denver song next, I grabbed the guitar and sang a song about why I didn't allow John Denver songs in my house. It came to me on the spot; I remember it had four verses, but that's all I remember about it. Something about Pat being there encourages shy people to be bold, and for those of us who are bold already, he encourages a wide-open wildness. Your tongue is loosened and you hear yourself being wittier than usual, sharper, happier.

Everybody who knows him has Pat Jobe stories. Mine include how he invited me to be on "Radio Free Bubba," how we had dinner with a gorgeous grandmother in leopard-print slacks, how I tell him sternly to quit preaching and he cheerfully ignores me, how we did a radio talk show in the window of the Sandwich Factory in downtown Spartanburg and sang "Christmas in Prison" for the audience, how we drove to the Promise Keepers' Clergy Rally at the Baptist church in Charlotte that's shaped like a giant pink crown, and in the lunch line Pat kept addressing me as "O Being of Light."

Those of you who can hear him on the radio know about his children, his adored wife Pam, the grandmother, the cats, the dogs, the fish and hamsters, the angels they make, and all the cacophony of family loving that their house holds. I don't know how they do it. I can't tell whether they are saints or crackpots. Probably, like most of us, they are some of each.

I'm happy to be in his world. I'm happy to get phone messages from him. One time he called, knowing I had just ended a job I loved, and that I didn't have any job after that. "I bet you can't hear the marching band on your front lawn," he said. "They are marching up and down playing 'Stars and Stripes Forever.'" He began playing mouth trumpet, sounding very much like a marching band.

"I can hear them now!" I said.

"Well, they will be playing out there for a while. They wanted to come play for you because of your extreme wonderfulness."

It works on me every time. Thanks, Pat.

Crying at the Movies

Kim Taylor

I cry at movies. Actually, that is an understatement. I don't drip a few tears. I really cry. I also really laugh, jump, fidget, growl, and grunt. But how much I cry, how hard I cry seem to be more impressive than those other reactions.

I saw the movie *White Oleander* with a group of women from work. These are women of heart, brain, and bone. I warned them I would cry. They said they would also cry. They dripped a few tears. I sobbed.

My friends were dear and sweet, petting me, rubbing my shoulders, hugging me. Maybe I should cry more often!

As I drove home after the movie, I wondered why I seem to cry so much harder than most anyone else I know at movies.

When I was a child, we watched Walt Disney's *Wonderful World of Color* every Sunday night. I always cried. Always. For the dogs. For the kids. For the old people. There was always someone to cry for. I cried for them.

My parents were disturbed by my crying at movies. I remember a discussion of it once. Something about me feeling more about movies than life.

Well, yes. Movies are safe to feel. In movies and books, I know the characters' fates are sealed. The people on paper and on screen don't need me. There is nothing I can do for them. I don't have to walk on water. I can sink into the emotion and feel. Just feel all there is to feel. I can let it wash over me, through me. I can ride it like waves. I will not drown. I will not die. And they are not real.

In the movies, unlike life, things are said that need to be said. There is a big picture. No clouds. No blur. No danger.

I do not have to shield myself. I cannot hurt them. They cannot hurt me. They will not use my reactions against me. I will not be chided for my tears or fears. I am not even there.

But as I sit here, almost three hours after the movie, I am still riding the wake.

I have to pace myself. I can't see another movie like this one for a while. I read *The Lovely Bones* by Alice Sebold over a month ago. I can't think much about it without being rocked to my core.

I am churned up. Like turning the compost, the heat and smells rise. And I write. I write from these feelings that will go back into hiding, back to sleep, back to safety.

Maybe I write to appease the feelings, like singing them to sleep. Maybe I write to make them real, because they only come out when it is not real.

Maybe all my emotions occasionally need to show themselves, stretch, and walk around a bit. And movies and books are like a group outing to a bar. They can dance in the safety of darkness.

I realize now of course, that I'm feeling the agitation. I'm angry. I'm glad I'm home alone. But the old anger stirs and burns and growls in my gut.

I am angry at the parents from this movie. How dare you be so self-centered? How dare you walk around in the world, crashing into things and not cleaning up after yourself?

And I'm back in my primary relationships. Mom and Dad. I am back in the old wounds. Slapped back to the old emotions. Regressed. Sadly, sadly I can slip right back. I can stand here. I can look around. And I can feel it as if it were new.

And gladly, joyously, I can see where I am. Like a room in my heart, I can stand here—and I can leave when I'm ready. Not slamming the door behind me. But closing it quietly. Leaning against it and resting. Laughing and crying.

The pain is so familiar. There is odd comfort in that.

I see the people on paper and on film, and I know someone else has a room like mine.

I Am an Idiot

Pat Jobe

I am an idiot. This needs to be on the record because when I am old, my children are going to be tempted to have me heavily drugged in some facility where they do that sort of thing. I'm asking you, my listeners of record, to keep this from happening. Here's why. I am now spacially challenged to the point that I sometimes wreck cars and I often get lost. This is very embarrassing to admit, but if I don't, in about the year 2030, there will be a meeting of my children at which the following will be said, "Dad went to pay the cable bill the other day and couldn't find the cable company. I'm afraid we're going to have to put him in one of those places where they give people lots of drugs."

One of you will have to come to that meeting and say, "Look here. I have the transcript of a radio commentary your dad did back in 1998, and just that day he had gone to try to pay his cable bill and couldn't find the cable company."

My gaggle of children will gather round the document that I now hold in my hand and scratch their chins and cut their eyes at each other, wonder what to do.

It is very important that you show up at the meeting with this piece of paper.

Here are your instructions:

1. If Mom is still living, get her to talk to him. She's always been great.

2. Feed him. He has always loved to eat.

3. Give him whatever he asks for. No, within reason, give him whatever he asks for.

4. Take him to a movie and remind him that to talk during a movie is rude.

5. Ask him if he would play you a song on his guitar. Help him find his guitar and tune it for him.

6. Get someone he likes to listen to him. Maybe you kids could take turns at this.

7. Come back and visit soon.

8. Give him whatever he asks for.

I don't mean by this piece to make fun of other people's problems. Rather I intend by this piece to encourage all my relatives and friends in making my old age an enjoyable and somewhat challenging time. I do not want to be thrown on the scrap heap of life without first being used by a purpose I perceive is a mighty one, to paraphrase George Bernard Shaw. I want to be old without boundaries, much as I try to do the mid-forties without boundaries, without subtlety, with malice toward none and charity for all. I intend to fight as an old man, unless, by some miracle, all the good fights are won. I will advocate for the voiceless, harvest for the hungry, and generally make an effective nuisance of myself so that people will help me just to get rid of me.

Huge parties, dances, great balloon decorations

and races, feasts for one and all are also on my agenda for the next sixty to eighty years. I plan to die as a very old man, holding hands with my soon-to-be-dead wife as we walk down a deserted beach and to have our bodies found by someone who won't be terribly upset, maybe a seasoned police officer or a shark who catches our bodies in the rising tide.

Regardless of how many of my dreams come true, your job is to be there when they try to lock me up for not being able to find the cable company. Remember, I was sane and competent when I couldn't find the cable company way back when, and I'll be sane and competent when I can't find the cable company again.

Sprains and Strains

Kim Taylor

I bought a house.

It is a nice little house that sits up on a ridge just at the edge of town. There is a little back porch from where I can drink coffee and gaze out at Mount Mitchell. The long narrow lot slopes down into a wooded gully. The new bypass is on the other side.

The whole process of buying the house, making all the arrangements—well, I'd forgotten all the maneuvering, the chess play, the magic of timing and pleading that must go on.

Alas, all the arrangements were made and moving day came.

And halfway through it, I fell and sprained my ankle. Reinforcements were called in. I was planted on the sofa and watched as boxes and furniture paraded by.

Eventually, someone noticed that I was going into shock. I was swept off to the hospital. I did not protest. That was when everyone began to worry.

The ER doctor was nice. He explained that I would not be moving anything for several weeks. I asked that he not tell me I'd have been better off to break it. "Well," he said.

"Please don't," I protested.

"At least you'd be able to walk out of here," he continued. "As it is, you won't be walking for at least two weeks. It is one of the worst sprains I've ever seen."

After cheering me up, he went off to get some drugs.

I'm older. I don't snap back like I used to.

There was so much to do. And I could do nothing.

The next weekend, I was supposed to go on a day trip to Asheville. A friend suggested we rent a wheelchair. And we did.

Asheville is a cool and groovy town. No one looked weirdly at our little band as we wheeled down the street.

But I had a cold hard crash course in "life in a wheelchair."

Bookstores, craft shops, card shops ... barely accessible.

And there was the wonderful little place we stopped for dinner. To use the bathroom, I had to go outside, down the street and be met at another door and re-enter the front of the building. I voted for hopping down the steps while my friend moved the wheelchair.

The sidewalks were tricky. The parking situation trickier. And there were lots of places I simply could not go.

For me, the situation was temporary. But I got a hard smack in my reality when I thought about the things I could not do, the places I could not go, the hip and interesting things I could not see from my perspective.

I really thought the world was a more accessible place. All the ramps. All the changes. But an inch or two makes an incredible difference.

Three little steps stood between me and the restroom. Fortunately, I was able to get up and hop those three steps. I had walked those steps before. I had never noticed there was no other way to the restroom.

I had never noticed how narrow the aisles are in most stores. I noticed as I backed out of the card shop and bookstore.

The clerks and salespeople were kind. They offered to move things around for me. Help me with this or that.

But it was such a big deal. Even just going to the bathroom took someone away from their post. Someone to unlock the doors. Someone to alter the norm.

Just an inch or two.

Rode Hard

Meg Barnhouse

You know, life is an inkblot.

Remember the Rorschach inkblot tests that psychologists give? You're supposed to say what the patterns make you think of. The old blots were one-color only, but now they are multi-colored. I had a friend who was getting her Ph.D. in psychology, and she decided to test me one day. I was having fun, entertaining myself. "Ooh, that one looks like two teenage girls in the deepest jungle holding hands and dancing around a cooking pot," I said. "This one¯it's what's left of a hotel room after two aliens have had a fight to the death."

She squinted at me and said, "Bats and butterflies, Meg. If anyone ever gives you this test, just say bats or butterflies."

But I digress. Life is like an inkblot in that you can tell a lot about another person by how they look at things that happen. Here are the events that led up to my writing this while I'm standing up because it hurts too much to sit down: I was at a friend's house on Lake Lure with my boys and one of their friends. We were playing in the water. The three teenage boys were diving, yelling, swimming, and floating. I was reading. They worked up their courage to jump off the second story of the boathouse, high above the water. Soon they were daring each other to perform twists and spins, to kick soccer balls while in the air.

I was reading. I looked up every time a boy plummeted from the roof above me into the water. Once in a while I would dive off the dock and swim around to cool off. Rainstorms were sweeping through the valley that day, so now and then we would get to swim among raindrops, which felt poetic.

The boys were having so much fun jumping off the second story of the boathouse, I decided I would do it, too. I remember walking up the steps, coming up onto the flat roof, looking down. The water looked far away, gleaming dully, metallic. My younger son said, "Oh, Mom, that's not a good idea. You might hurt yourself." His friend said, "Cool! Go! Go!" My oldest said, "She's going to do it anyway, just let her go."

I jumped. I meant to go in feet first, but something else happened. I hit sitting down. The impact felt like that paddle my first-grade teacher used on me once at Mulberry Street Elementary School. That's another story. I swam back to the dock with all the dignity I could muster. I didn't actually say, "Didn't hurt!" but I was attempting to convey that with my attitude. One time was enough, I told the guys, and I eased myself into the lounge chair to read for the rest of the afternoon.

It wasn't until the next day that I realized I had really hurt something. It felt like I was sitting on a tennis ball made out of bone. It was the kind of discomfort that builds until you can't think, and your vision narrows, and nothing outside of that feeling can really hold your attention. Anyway, so I've been dealing with it. For the past week or so, I have been noticing how much one sits down in the course of a life. I was shifting and grimacing in the hairdresser's chair. His sister asked how I had hurt myself. I told her I felt so good at the lake that I forgot I was in my late forties with a fifteen-year-old hip replacement and I got brave.

"Not brave, daredevil," the hairdresser's sister said, shaking her head at me.

"I don't see the difference," I said.

The doctor I finally went to said, "Hey, at least you had fun on the way down."

My chiropractor said, "You let your desire to hold onto your youth override your common sense, eh?"

It's funny how people see it differently. Getting

older takes some thinking about, and people seem to think about it in a couple of ways. Some people resign themselves to it early. They start talking about being old when they aren't old yet. Other people resist being old with every fiber of their will. Some people admire you when you don't act your age; others shake their heads. I'm trying to figure out where to stand in all of this, how to live gracefully in this body at this age.

My beloved said, "You're just you, and that's the way you do it."

Yep, foolish or brave, I use everything I've got pretty hard—my clothes, my car, my body. I will pretend to learn from this.

Life Is a Four-Letter Word

Pat Jobe

Why write? There are as many reasons as there are pieces of paper, even tablets of stone. There are as many reasons as there are emails flying through the World Wide Web, crisscrossing a zillion computers in a split second.

Why me? When I was young, I thought it would change the world. Now that my hair is gray and a young friend tells me I have scratches in my face, I hope to change myself.

And the changes that I hope to write into my

own mind and heart are not even changes other people will notice. I'm writing to change by degrees or percentages of degrees. I may note the slightest improvements.

Lately, I've asked myself for an essay a day, one gathering of between 400 and 450 words that might mark the passage of that one day, one thought, one memory, one image laid beside other images or discussed in the hallowed inner sanctum of the essayist with fingers on the keyboard, words lining up one behind the other on my computer screen.

My purpose is self-confrontation. What am I good for? Have more than five decades of middle-class, Southern luxury and consumption been worth the shotgun shell it would take to blow me to eternity? If I wander alone into the pasture behind my house, will I find anything worth bringing back to a reading public?

A flea just bit the inside of my right knee. He died for his sin. How much different from him am I? Can I write anything about fleas or fields or starlight or stagnation that has not already been written and read by better minds than mine?

Of course, I cannot. But I can bat. I can stare down pitches thrown my way and occasionally write about the ones that make an essay. We found a bullet hole in our office window and the bullet on the floor. I wrote about it. My daughter dropped out of college. I wrote about it. My six-year-old discussed sleeping and waking with me while I pumped gas and he felt the fuel jiggle through the hose.

A friend committed suicide and I cried on the phone with his mother. Life is full of ups and downs and turns and twists. I wrote about the D.C. sniper, an argument I had with my daughter over whether they serve pancakes at Waffle House, how my wife hates my arguing with my daughter.

Life is a four-letter word that contains everything from galaxies to mythological creatures. Part of mine being worth the shotgun shell involves sitting down and writing about it.

You Do It When You Do It

Meg Barnhouse

Spring is a time when everything comes around again, looking new, even though we have seen it before. Insights are like that, too. Sometimes they just have to bloom again, and you realize you had forgotten something that was really important, but here it is again. I just had one happen like that.

I have been in a serious writing slump. I haven't been doing enough nothing—just sitting around reading, or puttering in the yard. Those things free my mind up to write. I don't think that's the real reason, though. I've had church stuff to do, newsletter articles and tons of email and sermons, but that's not the real reason either. The real reason I haven't been writing is that—I haven't been writing. It has burst on me like a revelation. I do what I do, and I don't do what I don't do. I feel embarrassed by this, as if everyone on earth knows this but me. The way to write more is to turn on the computer, sit in front of it, and write.

Natalie Goldberg, whose books on writing I have read over and over, says she writes pages of something every morning, even if it's pages of "I don't know what to write, I can't think of a thing to write." In my mornings I get up, wake up my son, fix coffee, take him to school, go drink coffee with my friends, then go to work. I have acted like I couldn't write pages in the mornings, so I couldn't write.

I had a therapist who used to ask, when I said I couldn't figure out how to make something happen, "If I paid you a thousand dollars to figure it out, do you think you could?" An answer would spring to mind. "Yeah, of course, now if you paid me a thousand dollars, I could do it!" I heard his voice asking that question. I realized I can write pages anytime. That it is in sitting down and writing that I make writing happen. OH.

I know that this is the secret to eating right and exercising, too. I do what I do and I don't do what I don't do. I can plan to eat more fruit and vegetables. I can buy them at the store. That doesn't get it done.

I have to actually eat them instead of something else. I can plan to do exercise. I have planned to do yoga for about six years now. Last year I bought a mat. A friend made me some tapes. I am not feeling stretched out, strengthened, balanced. I may have to actually do the yoga to reap those benefits. If thinking about being healthy would make a person healthy, I would be walking around in a golden glow of health and good energy. People talk about getting their spiritual life going, but talking about it doesn't make it happen.

I do what I do and I don't do what I don't do. That's my new philosophy of life. My big insight. I think the Buddhists have been saying that for years. I vaguely remember learning something like that in my reading. But you know, reading something and realizing it in your belly are not the same thing. Anyway, it seems like the Buddhists get all the good insights first. It makes me feel a bit surly, if you must know. They are so dern calm and patient, and they do stuff like nod when you have a realization, and they don't say things like, "See, I've been trying to tell you that all along!"

But I digress. I was talking about writing, so I'm going to sit down and do it now. I have heard this somewhere before. Oh yeah, that's what I tell people when they say they want to be writers. It happens like this: Some people, when they find out I'm a writer, say something like, "I know I have at least one novel in me, I just have to let it out." "Sit down and do it!"

I say. Sometimes they think that is encouragement. It is, in a way. But it's also a declaration of hopelessness, a sure knowledge that the odds are good that they will wait for inspiration. That's a sure way not to write anything. Or they will wait until the house is cleaned up, or until they have a studio set up, or a new computer. Those are sure ways not to write anything. I know, I've tried them all. Sitting down and doing it is the secret to writing. This morning I remembered that.

Wish someone would pay me a thousand dollars.

Bad Dog

Kim Taylor

I have a bad dog.

At first glance, you would say to me, "What a pretty dog." She looks like a miniature black lab. Her eyes are bright and alert, and she seems always to be smiling.

Make no mistake, she is a bad dog. If she were a person, she'd have a diagnosis—probably sociopath. But you wouldn't see that. Only her bright eyes and cute white freckles.

She would be very careful with you—carefully hiding her dark side.

One of my many dog-loving friends accused me

of being far too harsh with this obviously sweet dog. But once, while I was away, I left the dog-lover to care for the sociopath. Upon my return, she stated she would never again be left alone with this dog.

I have a friend who is a vet. She is very kind to animals and very wise about their behaviors. I tried to describe the badness to the vet. She decided to come visit with my dog.

"What do you think?" I asked. "A little puppy Prozac?"

"Euthanasia," she answered calmly.

I laughed because I thought she was kidding.

"Nope," she said, "this dog is a knucklehead."

"Is that your official diagnosis?"

"Knucklehead," she answered.

According to the vet, some dogs are just bad dogs. No cure, no treatment, not even puppy Prozac will improve the condition.

So, after one of my friends has experienced the dark side, they inevitably ask me why I don't just get rid of her.

"How would I do that?" I ask. "I've got this really bad dog, do you want her? She chases cars, won't come when you call her and is constantly trying to alpha every living creature that comes through my door. She sees niceness as a sign of weakness. So if you are nice to her, she'll knock you down trying to get out the door. You sure you don't want her? See how cute she is? She'll smile at you after she knocks you down."

Once I got lectured from a passing car. Pyscho-pup had escaped. She was chasing cars. I was trying to recapture her. I have learned that I have to be nonchalant about it. I was strolling around my yard when a woman stopped her car in front of my house. She began scolding me for not having my dog put up. I explained that I was trying to put her up but that I had not been able to catch her.

The woman drove slowly down the road, calling in a high-pitched voice, "Here puppy, puppy, puppy." Then she backed the car back up the road and stopped again in front of my house. "She won't come when you call her," she said, incensed.

"Yes, ma'am," I answered, "she is a very bad dog. You want her?"

Incredible Journey Lite

Meg Barnhouse

Our two dogs live in a great yard. They can run, chase balls, catch Frisbees, bark at squirrels, run up the stairs to the deck, stick their heads through its rails. From there they are able to survey their domain and Max's. Max is the German Shepherd who lives on a chain in the yard next door. His domain is large, but he can't reach much of it. I don't know if our dogs feel sorry for him or if they feel lucky when they compare situations. Our dogs get fed everyday, with all the water they can drink. They have cow hoofs to chew on and three shade trees. Why would they want to be anywhere else?

Last week they pushed though the gate, which had been not-so-carefully shut. I came home after work and found them gone. I have never had dogs before. I'm really a cat person. Cats roam, and then they come back. I didn't know if you could count on dogs to do that. In movies I have seen people out in cars looking for dogs. You can learn a lot about what to do in life from the movies, so I got in the car and rode slowly around, whistling and calling them out the window of the car. All through the neighborhood dogs answered my whistles, but there was no sign of our two.

I drove around to the neighborhood beside us, and to the one across the creek behind us, but no one had seen a German Shepherd puppy and an old Aussie shepherd limping, leaping, and quarreling, which is mostly what they do together. I talked to people who were also just home from work, but they hadn't seen anything. I talked to little kids, who see everything, but they hadn't seen our dogs either. I called and left a message with Animal Control and with the shelter.

When my sweetheart came home, we did the whole thing all over again, except I learned I should have driven around quietly, listening for the barking of other dogs, which would tell us where ours were. Into the evening, we interviewed people of all ages, races, and levels of intoxication. No dogs.

Back at home, there was a message on the phone. Animal Control had picked up the dogs at three o'clock that afternoon. They were at the shelter. Why had I not checked the machine? As I said, I'm a cat person. No one calls you when your cat runs away. The shelter was closed when we finally got the phone message, so we went the next morning to spring the girls from lockup. After paying $55 per animal reclaiming fee, and $20 per animal microchipping fee, we were dead broke. In addition to that, we had one ticket per dog for $150 each because they were running loose, and another ticket (same amount) because one dog had an old rabies tag on¯even though the vet's office vouched for her shots being up-to-date.

I would understand getting a ticket for the third time your animals were out. I would understand a $20 reclaiming fee. I hear, telling this story, that some families who find their lost pets at the shelter these days can't afford to get them back. They leave the animal there, to be adopted by another family, or to be euthanized. That bites, so to speak. There was a tiny Betta fish on the desk left by an owner who wouldn't pay the $55 bucks to get it back. Someone said it had been confiscated in a law enforcement raid, along with twenty nine fighting chickens. It looked part forlorn, part ticked-off.

Our dogs had been picked up on a road about five miles from our house, across the interstate. I know the bridge they crossed. It's a narrow two-lane with SUVs barreling across it. It was like that Disney movie, only with a shorter trip, a kind of *Incredible Journey* Lite. Plus, our dogs would never have found their way home.

We lectured them on the way back to the house, our now very expensive dogs. They had the smarts to look remorseful. I told them I don't understand why, if you love your people and they feed you and you see your alternative life on a chain next door, you would run away. Maybe that's part of dogginess. Lots of people find dogs charming. I will again. Give me time.

Yard Sale Religion

Pat Jobe

I've discovered a secret religion here in our sacred Southland. My revealing its practice will not affect it because no one will admit that it's a religion. If you confront one of them directly, even in the midst of their practice, they'll look at you like you're crazy. The secret is sealed.

So don't let on you know. Just practice their

religion with them. Or not. It's that kind of religion. It is practiced by people who hold yard sales on the side of the road.

The basic ideas of the religion are that God loves everybody and nobody is really screwing up all that badly. The intricacies and codes of the religion are literally countless, but scholars of this faith can read many of these codes in the piles of clothing, old toys, broken lawn mowers, even the shapes formed by the shade of the trees under which these sales take place. Let me give an example. You stop your car and approach a pale woman with ill-fitting clothes, a tattoo, and like myself, lacking a few teeth.

You say, "How you doing?" In the code of the yard sale religion, which has a secret unpronounceable name, you are saying, "The Buddha himself was not more beautiful than you. Your ill-fitting garb, your teeth, your tattoo, all of it hides the beauty of your soul, the power of your heart, your ability to spread glory in every moment." She says back, "Fine. Hi you?" The code translates, "Your infinite soul shines from every pore of your skin. All that is holy is manifested in your balding, beer-bellied body and the seriousness with which you gaze upon the discarded clothing of my children and my chipped coffee mugs."

And, of course, the items in the yard sale are all sacred. A chipped coffee mug with blue flowers painted on the side symbolizes the determination of

God to penetrate our hearts with love, great dancing, and steaming strong drinks. “How much you want for ’at mug?” you ask her, and the code is, “Deep emotional healing comes with every breath. Mental health and world peace lie one step from here. Come let us step together.”

“A dime,” she says flatly, but the flat tones of her voice are the highly-trained chants of a yard-sale priestess. Her message is, “The steps are simple and the way is clear. Let us all be one in breaking walls and healing our hearts into the one heart.” You look at her, confident that the two of you are part of a larger dance, a beautiful ride on the seesaw of eternity. She is enraptured to hear you ask, “Would you take a nickel?”

Temple of the DMV

Meg Barnhouse

Early in the morning, Spartanburg, South Carolina. We are a mother and a son waiting together. This is an important day. The feeling is of sitting in the temple of a solemn religion. Young men and women of the region come to this temple with their hearts, their futures, their well-being held in trembling hands. They are here for a rite of passage. The tests are difficult. The stakes are high. We are at the Department of Motor Vehicles, waiting to take the drivers license test.

The atmosphere is hushed, heavy with portent. If you are deemed worthy, you may cross the threshold into adulthood. You will have freedom, motion, independence. The priestesses move slowly but with purpose behind a waist-high wall. An amplified voice calls overhead in measured tones: "Now serving number 315 at window twelve. Number 315 at window twelve."

Obstacles have been set and overcome. We have had the proper preparatory classes. Tests of eyesight and memory have been completed. We have the right pieces of paper. As in the old stories where the young ones are told to gather one feather from the phoenix that flies out of the east on winter solstice, one berry from the bush that sits high on the west side of yonder mountain, one vial of water from the dew on the first rose of summer. We have the correct insurance information. We have the right dates on our applications. We have had the permit for the required length of time. All is in order.

Parents sit nearby their young men and women, trying to be encouraging without being intrusive. Allowing the young people to retain their essential coolness, which is, after all, what they believe will take them through the test. Did they study the book? In this religion, study of the book is essential. They don't always do it, though, believing that their coolness will carry them farther than it actually will. Did they practice? Some got behind the wheel and pulled into the space between the two sawhorses at the high school, parallel-parking until they were masterful. Some did not. Some studied the book but did not practice driving. Some have driven in the fields since they were thirteen but have not opened the book.

Then the time is at hand. The tester comes to gather your young person, to take them to the threshold, to put him or her through the test of knowledge, skill and endurance. Some testers seem to want the young person to do well. Some smile when the young person forgets to pull up the emergency brake when parking as if for the whole night. The tester smiles when the young person pulls around a bicyclist as she has seen her father do time and time again. This young person fails the test.

If the young people fail, will they lower their heads and acknowledge that they should have practiced, that they should have studied the book? Probably not. They will blame the tester. They may utter angry words and make fearsome gestures. They may cry. Maybe this shows they don't yet have the maturity to cross the threshold. Maybe this is how the parent behaves as well. Maybe the parent resolves to work harder on character formation, on correct behavior. Maybe it is too late. They wrestle together with the issues raised by the trials they have passed through. The threshold will be approached again.

If the young people pass the test, there is feasting and celebration. There are solemn speeches about responsibility and heartfelt congratulations. Another one is launched. The opponents have been worthy, as has been your young one. Adulthood is one step closer. One must mark these thresholds with care and attention. Amen.

Mayday, Mayday

Kim Taylor

Today, Ms. McGillicutie, who is now eleven and a half, informed me that she would not be walking to class with Scooter and me. I asked if it was because we are not cool enough. She laughed. I informed her that there are no two cooler people on the planet. She smiled.

Ms. McGillicutie is in a phase of development that is most confusing. Last night at a ballgame, she sat with me. She never sits with me at ballgames. She actually put her head on my shoulder and talked to me. She never does this in public. I wanted to grab her little head and kiss it. But I had to act as though I was not overwhelmed with joy and love. I had to pretend that this cuddling was an everyday event. Nothing out of the norm. Nothing to MAKE A BIG DEAL ABOUT, OKAY?

Then less than twelve hours later, she can't be seen with me in public. She scurries away from us in the parking lot claiming she must hurry to class—even though we are ten minutes earlier than usual.

I am constantly reminding myself not to take this personally. I am also constantly reminding her that her sister and I are not something she needs to scrape off the bottom of her shoe.

She loves me, she hates me, she loves me, she hates me. I'm invisible.

I'm confused.

I know my job here is like that of the chair judge at a tennis match. No matter how much like John McEnroe she acts, I need to remain calm and firm. The call is the call. Like it or hit the shower. Don't engage. Don't react.

I know this. I am just really lousy at it.

She knows where all my buttons are.

All she has to do is grunt and roll her eyes and suddenly I'm standing and screaming. And feeling like a perfect idiot.

I would love to blame hormones—hers or mine. I'd love to blame my parents, my diet or global warming. I would love for her to just behave the way I want her to. I would love a pill that would calm me or one that would straighten her out.

But dammit, this involves self control. My self-control. I really hate that.

I am getting advice about how to handle this

phase of our development. Unfortunately, there are no helpful hints about how to put the good advice into practice. Nothing other than counting to ten before I speak.

So now I'm trying to figure out how to install an early warning system. Mayday. Mayday. Red alert. System failure is imminent.

I'm looking for that step in-between implosion and ejecting the warp core. I need to drive a wedge in that split second between her eye rolling and my screaming.

I need to find the black box. The cockpit voice recorder.

I need to alter the system so that this kind of failure is not repeated.

All systems need to be in perfect working order. We are about to enter uncharted territory. Black holes and plasma streams are inevitable. Alien life forms will be encountered.

I must alter my command strategies. I must stop watching so much "Star Trek."

I am entering a confusing stage in my own development.

Cussing

Meg Barnhouse

I guess my oldest child got it from me, this love of cussing. For most of my life I have tried to speak in pleasant words, well-grounded words. Then I started hanging out with a couple of cussing people. I'm not going to name names, but I'm blaming this squarely on them. I mean, I'm all for taking responsibility for my own character defects, but only when I'm forced to do it.

When this child was three and a half, we started toilet training. I thought and thought about a way to make it appealing to him to sit there in the bathroom waiting for something to happen. One day when I was having to scold him about using dirty words, you know, three-year-old dirty words, like poo-poo and pee-pee and bottom, I had an inspiration. Kneeling down to get to eye level, I held his hands in mine and said, "Honey, those are words you can only use when you are sitting on the potty. In fact, when you are sitting on the potty, you may say them as much as you want, or you could even make up a song entirely from potty words."

His eyes lit up. From there on out, the training went like a dream. We would sit together, I on the edge of the tub, he on the throne, and we would sing "Pee-pee pee-pee, poo-poo bottom," and we would laugh uproariously. Neither of us could believe we were getting away with what we were getting away with.

Later on, when he was eleven, he said something was crap. Now, in Philadelphia, I grew up not knowing that was a bad word. My dad, who never cussed in my presence (except once when I was fifteen, but that's another story) said things were crap all the time. Again, struck by a dubious inspiration, I said, "You're not allowed to say 'crap' until you're twelve." People in my generation, the baby boomers, don't seem to want to grow up because the grown-ups forgot to make being grown-up look appealing. They said things like "enjoy this while you can, because when you grow up, you'll have to worry about paying bills and taxes and being responsible."

I figured I needed to make getting older have some appeal. In the spirit of that moment, I thought cussing was something that would make it feel cool to reach twelve, maybe balance out my rule that kids had to start doing their own laundry at twelve as well. On his twelfth birthday, this came back to haunt me. "I'm happy as crap to be twelve," he crowed, "get away from me!" This to his younger brother: "You are full of crap!" "Mom, this cake is crap-a-licious!" You can imagine how tired I was of that word after just one day. Then, at thirteen, fourteen, and fifteen he wanted another word allowed.

At fifteen, it was "hell." I figure people even say that one in some churches. The ministers, especially. I won't say what words my son is now allowed, at sixteen, to use. He uses good judgment about where and when to use the words, after the actual day of his birthday. No, he is still not allowed to say the mother of all cuss words. Eighteen. I knew that was your next question.

I'm trying to cut way back on my cussing, especially since now I'm working in a church, and it takes people aback when their minister doesn't speak pleasantly. They are a loving and forgiving group, but I don't want to put that to the test very often. Sometimes, though, it satisfies the soul and makes the heart light to just cut loose. In the car, all alone, with the windows rolled up. Because, you all know, the car is where you're allowed to say all those words. However, if the thought of a minister cussing is offensive to you, and if you see me on the road with my mouth moving, I'm singing along with the radio. That's my story and I'm sticking to it.

The Well-Thrown Fit

Pat Jobe

In a recent piece, I offered two ways to handle hard times. One is to stay with it 'til it's over, and the other, not recommended, is to use addictions: sex, violence, drugs, alcohol, junk food, or television.

Driving among the cow pastures and hills of Upstate South Carolina, I noticed three more ways: anger, joy, and the well-thrown fit. The well-thrown fit is not far from anger, but I separate them because one is more grown-up and boring and offensive.

Anger is not only grown-up and boring, but it is also my most-often-chosen and humiliating way. The slow burn, the sulking pout, the private tirade, the sarcastic remark, the full-blown holler, and the slammed fist into the steering wheel are all symptoms of anger, anger, anger.

I once met with nurses at Rutherford Hospital. They said their most common emergency room injury is a "boxing injury," generally caused by men putting their fists through walls. That is their most common injury. Yikes.

The well-thrown fit is demonstrated by various members of my family, most recently my three-year-old, Luke. It looks more out of control, like a hurricane or a leak in the plumbing, but it's clear that a three-year-old has as much control of his fit as I do over my fist in the steering wheel. Either of us can cut it off quickly. The well-thrown fit appeals because I'm no good at it. I'm too cussed male, grown-up—I despise confessing all this—but I really am too grown-up to holler and cry and stamp my little foot, or even better, roll in the floor.

Finally, there's joy. The ancients say we are to rejoice in all things, but we answer, "Yeah, right," and move on to the next opportunity to slam a steering wheel or roll around in the floor hollering and crying.

Still, joy is a choice. I noticed it as the cow pastures and fluffy white clouds passed my car windows. Things were not good or bad in my life. I was having a multi-layered morning. One level of me felt chipper and optimistic. Another floor was mired in grief and worry, and down a third hallway, frustration tap-danced with resolution when I remembered my life is over-populated. Yes, there is romance in too many dogs, cats, and children, but there's also insanity, and the two tend to spar.

And in the midst of all my whining self-pity, a chipper belief survives that dreams really do come true. The universe began to pulse with this woompa, woompa that I hear of late, this transcendent truth that beyond the beyond there really is joy that cannot be undone. It's almost like command and control, central casting, whoever is in charge shows up with flowers and the perfect wine and says, "I love you, sweetheart. Let's go dancing."

Woompa. Woompa.

Endless Decent

Meg Barnhouse

Every time I see the torn ticket from the punk extravaganza, I smile. I keep it in the section of my pocketbook where my cell phone goes, so I see it pretty often. I came back from that concert with a fake black leather bracelet on each arm. One had seven silver rings on it, the other had a row of skulls. My nails were painted green. My teenaged sons were elated.

We had spent the day at the Vans Warped Tour. One punk band after the other had played on five stages. Lots of times you could hear three of them going at once. A crowd of kids, mostly teenagers, mostly dressed in black, flowed from stage to stage seeing The Starting Line, The Ataris, Messd, Simple Plan, and some other ones I had not heard of. Vendors in booths sold bracelets with skulls on them, hemp necklaces, sunglasses, and water.

The temperature hovered around ninety degrees. The sun beat down on the crowd with no cloud cover and no shade. The place had a no-smoking, no-drinking policy. This was very different from the rock concerts I had gone to as a teen. Maybe everything the punk kids need comes in a pill. I did see a couple of kids sitting, leaning against a wall here and there, looking—um—tired. Maybe they were high. Maybe it was heat exhaustion. The only obvious crime I saw being committed was the vendors charging $3.50 for a small bottle of water.

I spent part of the day inside the "reverse day care" tent. This was the location where kids could drop off their parents. They had headphones for us, free ice water, folding canvas chairs, and piped-in cool air. I sat in the back, sipping cool water, reading a murder mystery, with foam earplugs wedged into my ears. Playing in a rock band in college damaged my ears. I don't want to risk more. I gave my sons earplugs to wear. One of them did wear them, for a while. I think. On the other side of the tent's canvas was a stack of speakers for one of the stages. The music coming out of the speakers had a bass beat that thumped its way through my bones, down to my toes. Usually I like the feeling of loud music and drums rattling my bones, but after five hours I began to think it might be enough.

The main thing that struck me about the kids that day was how nice they were. Sure, lots of them looked like they fell face first into a tackle box. There were rings on fingers, in eyebrows, pierced noses and tongues, ears and lips. The f-word was the most common adjective. You know what, though? If you were in the middle of the mosh pit, the crowd of kids bumping around like overheated molecules in front of the stage, and if you pointed your thumbs up and shouted, "I wanna go UP," then a couple of big guys would lift you so you could launch yourself and be passed hand to hand, shoulder to shoulder, crowd surfing. Sure, you got dropped sometimes. But someone would notice, reach down and help you up, ask if you were okay.

All the black clothes and the scary-looking hair and decoration reminded me of this car I saw cruising in Chesnee, South Carolina, one Sunday afternoon. Lots of kids have lettering across the back windshield saying "no fear," or "fear this." They want to look tough and scary. This one muscle car had, in gothic letters across the back, "Endless Descent." Anyway, that's what he meant to say. They had left out one "s," so what it ended up saying was "endless decent." Yeah, they can't help it. They're Carolina kids. Dressed in black, with lip rings and a mohawk, still say "yes ma'am" to their mamas when they're in trouble, still help you up when you go down in the mosh pit. We're going back to the concert next summer. Maybe I'll try some crowd surfing next time.

September 11, 2001

Kim Taylor

On September 11, 2001, I was in my office in the McDowell County Administration building. There was a meeting of the Criminal Justice Partnership Program scheduled for 10 a.m. at the coffee shop down the street. I was looking forward to the break. I love the new coffee shop. And I have known the women who are on this board for many years. They are strong and intelligent with big old mushy hearts.

I cut through the courthouse and picked up my old pal, Patti. We strolled up the street admiring the blue sky and cool morning. We talked about what a great idea it was to have the meeting at the coffee shop instead of downstairs in one of the boardrooms.

But when we topped the stairs, the look on the faces of our colleagues stopped us cold. They tried to fill us in, but at that point there was more speculation and rumor than fact. We sat huddled around a table trying to have a meeting and watch the television screen at the same time. When one head turned, all heads followed.

We saw the second plane hit. We watched the towers come down.

There was little business done at this meeting. Still, we had a hard time leaving. We all shuffled back to our offices.

I went home for lunch and watched the news.

That night, I tried to calm my children's fears. What would a war mean? Would we all become slaves to this man with the funny name?

Those are the monsters under their beds. Like all parents, I tried to shine light there. I tried to explain their fears away.

My fears have not been as easily dismissed.

I don't fear for democracy, the economy, or personal freedom. I do worry about the use of the word "war." I remember the Vietnam conflict all too well. I find myself torn between my belief in peace and the memory of the twin towers full of people turned to rubble.

I think of a crazed man with a sledgehammer some twenty or so years ago taking whacks at Michelangelo's Pieta.

I am not comparing the devastating loss of life on 9/11/01 to the damage done to a work of art. I'm thinking about how in one moment, one individual can cut so deeply into all our souls.

That is the monster under my bed.

Stairway to Heaven

Meg Barnhouse

What makes a perfect moment?

I found myself in the middle of one last October at the county fair. My twelve-year-old son and I and our friend Robin had just staggered off that ride that slings you sideways until your neck is bent and your stomach and kidneys are rubbing up against each other for the first time in your life. We walked in circles for a minute trying to decide whether we were going to need to throw up or not. When we didn't, we decided it must be a good time for a hot dog at Biker Barbie's. We lined up at the counter on black leather motorcycle seats that weren't quite level. Or maybe it was an inner-ear thing. You had to pay attention not to slide off. The hot dogs were good, and only something like $13.50 apiece.

The temperature was perfect. Mid-October, late afternoon, a slight chill in the air. Robin and I decided the Ferris Wheel was definitely next. My son declined. He would be slung around to within an inch of his life, but he did NOT think the Ferris Wheel looked fun. "Mom, they stop you up there," he said, pointing at the cars swinging high in the sky.

"Yeah!" I said. "You can see everything from there." He shuddered. We waited in line for a while and then it was our turn to load up into a car. It was yellow, and it swung as we got in. The ride operator was playing Led Zeppelin. We began to circle around, the music sounding loudest at the platform, fading as we swung upwards. Then our car stopped. I could see my boy on the ground, ball cap, baggy pants, hands in his pockets. He pulled one out to give a little wave. The sun was going down out behind the railroad yard. Flags of all colors were snapping in the breeze down below over the rides and games. It all looked so normal.

A month before, terrorists had attacked our country, shaking our sense of ourselves, our feeling of what life was like for us. It was something the rest of the world has known for a long time, but we have been able to remain unaware. Security is a superstition. It could all go any minute. And yet there was this life to be lived. The chill in the air, the sunset, my son waving, this moment rang like a temple bell. Ordinary life is what is most to be desired. To love, to be with friends, to continue on with the dailiness of it. I could see it all from here. We must not be afraid. The song wafted up: "… and she's buying a stairway to heaven … " I was in it. Heaven filling up and overflowing. I wish the possibility of that moment for people all over the world.

Twin Towers One Year Later

Pat Jobe

American flags on the backs of firetrucks—I don't remember seeing that before September 11, 2001. "God Bless America" has now been printed an additional hundred million times on bumper stickers, restaurant marquees, and car magnets from Florida to Alaska.

We have killed many of those we believe were somehow responsible for killing more than three thousand of our countrymen on this tragic morning last year, along with many other innocents who could not pronounce Al Qaeda, World Trade Center, or

George W. Bush. Soldiers wearing the uniforms of a dozen countries, including our own, have killed and died. And does anyone believe anything is any different? Does anyone believe those with the skill and the mindset to do it will not do it again?

One thing for certain is different. Afghan women are walking the streets of their towns and cities with more freedom than they once had. They are again conducting business, teaching school, doctoring and leading government agencies in a country where the Taliban confined them to their homes and state mental hospitals during its reign of terror.

And dissenters are not beheaded in the soccer stadium on Friday afternoons anymore. But Afghanistan is still a rough place to be a woman, and not that easy a place to be a man. America is still a rough place to be a woman, and not that easy a place to be a man, especially a man or woman of integrity, compassion, peace, grace, generosity, or forgiveness.

That is what is so cursed about this whole thing for me. I feel powerless and insipid in the face of the war on terrorism. There will be a terrible harvest of bloodshed followed by more bloodshed as long as we continue to live by the sword. The oldest teachings on record tell us this.

So there you go. We are doomed to swing the big stick and swing it and swing it. Peace is not possible until the bad guys are killed or put in prison. The only problem is the world cannot agree on who the bad guys are, and on both sides, their mothers and fathers keep giving the world their sons. You will hear a great deal today about fallen heroes, and God knows, there are many. But today is not just about remembering the fallen heroes. Today is also about remembering that war is a sick concoction of the human soul, and every death at the hands of war is a sad and sickening waste of creativity and love and potential. I am so sorry.

Compassion

Kim Taylor

On and off over the past twenty-five years, I've worked in the court system. My jobs have all been human services jobs of one kind or another. Most recently, I've worked for an alternative sentencing program. I explain it to my clients like this: I'm writing a research paper about you. I'll give the paper to the judge the day you go to court. Then the judge gets to read the story of who you are, how you got here, and what I think it will take to keep you from coming back.

In this line of work, I have met some very damaged people who have caused a great deal of damage themselves. I have worked with people whose strength and resilience have surprised me. I have worked with people whose depravity has appalled me.

And I have learned a little something about compassion.

The man had been in jail for months. He was charged with committing a heinous crime against a child. Every time I saw him, he was crying.

Law enforcement folks saw him as manipulative. Mental health folks saw him as severely depressed. I did not know how to see him.

He was found competent to stand trial.

On the day of his trial, he was brought to court in shackles, never having made bond. He began to cry shortly after his arrival. By the time his case was called, he was having a hard time holding his head up.

The officer stood and gave her report to the court of the events surrounding the charges and the confession of the accused. The attorney stood and reported how shocked the man's co-workers had been to learn of the charges. The judge began reading my report.

I watched the man cry. From the corner of my eye, I saw one of the clerks wave a tissue in the direction of the bailiff. He shook his head, "No." I handed my papers to the probation officer beside me, walked to the clerk, retrieved the tissue and walked across to the man. I put the tissue in his hand and squeezed his arm. I went back to my seat.

I did not feel the floor under my feet. I did not feel my body in the chair. I did not feel myself make the decision to make that walk. I am sure that the experience could not be replicated in a laboratory. There was no music. No blinding lights. Just a few seconds in my life when everything around me changed.

Whatever had happened, whatever would happen was outside this moment. In this moment, I was the person I always wanted to be.

Two-Rainbow Day

Pat Jobe

Rainbows make me believe in a god. I say "a god," because I have lived long enough to know that almost no two people mean the same thing when they use the word "god." How in the world they have organized religions beats me senseless, but then it often appears that religions have very little to do with god, and any decent god would have little to do with them.

But I just can't see a rainbow without uttering breathlessly, "Thank you, God."

Or sometimes I sound like a teeny bopper, "Oh my god."

On July 29, I had a two-rainbow day. As I was leaving my camper in Goose Creek, South Carolina, I saw a rainbow over the marsh, the same marsh that was once populated by twenty-eight herons standing like sentinels over a mystical domain. I whooped and prayed and hollered and cheered. I tried to simultaneously utter every sacred sound I had ever heard in my life. It didn't work, of course, but it gives you an inkling of just how rabid I can become over a rainbow.

The rest of the day went well. I drove about four hundred miles from Goose Creek to Summerville to Walterboro to Beaufort to Jasper County and back up I-95 to I-26, a quick stop in Columbia, a surprising phone call wherein someone said something nice to me, and home to Chesnee.

As I approached the Cowpens National Battlefield on Piedmont Road in Cherokee County, the second rainbow arched across the evening sky and sent me into babbling brooks of revelry. I knew I was the luckiest man on the face on the earth, with all due respect to Lou Gehrig. That night I heard Alexandra Kerry say that her father had told her being alive and being American makes us the luckiest people.

No, no. With a heart full of patriotism and love for my country, I must insist it is simply to live that makes us lucky. And I expect the dead find that funny. But I could be wrong about that.

Field Trip

Meg Barnhouse

The fifth-grade kids in the back of the Rambler station wagon felt Mama downshift to give the engine more power up the steep curve. It threw us forward a little and jostled us against each other. Three of us were not in the back seat, we were in the WAY back. I fell against my best friend Pam, and she fell against Clifford Scoggins, which was a scream.

Mama was teaching fifth grade that year. I was in fourth. My sister was only in second, so she couldn't go. Clifford was in Mama's class, even though he was every bit of fourteen years old. He had been held back several times at Mulberry Elementary School in Statesville, North Carolina. This was his second year in Mama's class. She said his family fed their children an RC Cola and a Moon Pie for breakfast. She said his dad was a sorry cuss, and that was all she was going to say about that. Mama told good stories, kind-of nice and kind-of mean at the same time. I'm not sure how she did that, but we laughed all the time at the dinner table.

Even though I was only in fourth grade, in Miss Foster's class, Mama had said I could come on the fifth-grade field trip and I could bring Pam. We were driving up into the mountains, onto the Blue Ridge Parkway. All the teachers were driving, and some parents were driving, too. I told you already we were in the way back of Mama's blue Rambler station wagon. We waved at the kids in the car behind us and made faces for a while, but how long can a person do that and have fun?

Mama played the radio for us, even though probably some of the class parents would fuss because it was devil music. Top 40. It was 1964. Pam could sing "I Wanna Hold Your Hand," and she sounded EXACTLY like the Beatles on the radio. The Beatles were new. Their music shone like candy. It was worldly, foreign but somehow familiar. Like I was almost remembering the words and the tunes when they sang them, even though I hadn't heard them before. Like there was a place in that music for me if I could figure out how to get in. That spring, I wasn't in yet, but it felt like it was right around the corner. Pam was in, yeah, definitely, she was there. Pam and I were singing, "And when I touch you I feel happy inside. It's such a feeling that my love, I can't hide …" It made my heart feel all opened up and smiling.

Clifford looked at her sideways, squinting one eye, smiling crookedly with his lips together. He was way too cool to sing, but he could express appreciation without risking being one of us little kids. One strand of his sandy hair had worked loose of the hair cream, and it curved over his pale freckly forehead. Pam had red hair, and she wasn't smiling while she sang because it was real important to her to remember each and every word just right. Her British accent was perfect, I thought. We used to ride horses together out at her house and sing and talk about who we were going to be when we grew up and we'd play redcoat spies and she was a double agent against the British because she could talk like they did. I was George Washington.

When we got out of the cars to look at some old-timey cabins up on the Blue Ridge Parkway, Mama and the other teacher talked to us about how the people lived, told us we should imagine living in those cabins, having to hunt and fish for food, carry water from the stream, keep the fire going all winter long like they did in *Little House on the Prairie.* We were riding the horses in our mind, going to get water. We were thinking what it would be like to have a husband waiting at the cabin, manly and smooth. We couldn't picture what he would do exactly, but he was around the place. Clifford amused us by hammering a quarter into a wooden fence post. He used his shoe for the hammer. I thought he was a little like Elvis, only with sandy hair. It was the coolest day.

Cell Phone Drivers

Kim Taylor

I have been hearing more and more complaints about people driving while using their cell phones. Not all people who use cell phones while operating a motor vehicle are a menace. However, some people can't walk and chew gum at the same time.

I heard Phyllis Diller say years ago (for those of you who don't know who Phyllis Diller is, I hate you more than words can say) that she was such a bad driver that she had to park the car to blow the horn.

If you are that bad at driving, I hope you know it. But I knew a very dear sweet woman who insisted on reading magazines while she drove. She never knew where she was or how she got there. But her most frightening trait was needing to make eye contact with whomever she was talking to while she was driving. Front seat. Back seat. It did not matter. The thought of this woman with a cell phone makes my heart stop.

I have another friend who was stuck in her car for almost twenty minutes once. She had dropped the pen she'd borrowed from the drive-in window of the bank. The pen had fallen down beside the seat. She was able to get hold of the pen, but unable to remove her hand while holding the pen. It took the bank manager coming outside and offering the pen as a gift for her to remove her hand and drive away. We must never let her have a cell phone.

I, too, have been tooling along the highway only to get behind someone who was doing forty-five miles per hour one minute and eighty the next. Upon passing the vehicle, I would see the driver chattering away on a cell phone.

Trust me, I feel your pain.

On the other hand, I have to visit people in their homes as part of my day job. I need my cell phone to locate people after their very careful directions leave me miles from nowhere. Occasionally, I operate my cell phone while driving my car. Wow, I feel like I've just confessed a crime.

Okay, here is my solution—we license people to drive with the phones. Like you have a special endorsement on your license: able to operate a motor vehicle while using a mobile cellular telephone.

Already you have to have special endorsements to operate motorcycles, drive eighteen-wheelers or wear glasses when you drive. So we just make it part of the test. You must drive with a license examiner present and pull your phone out of your briefcase, backpack or purse, dial the number and actually talk to another living being for at least two minutes without veering, altering your speed or generally screwing up.

I think this is a fair test. It is obvious from my many hours on the highway that far too many people are awarded the privilege to drive as it is. Instead of a privilege, they think it is a birthright. That all lanes coming and going belong only to them and speed is at their discretion—not mine as it should be. They park in places where they shouldn't, throw crap from their car window and play really bad music way too loud.

Now, if you'll excuse me, I have to drive to court in the next county to pay off my traffic ticket. I think I'll make a few phone calls on the way.

Mind Wash

Meg Barnhouse

Are you the kind of person who gets songs stuck in your head? I am. Now and then I get a song as pushy and rude as a professional wrestler before the big show, shouting down all normal brain activity. I can try to have a conversation on the phone or help my third-grader with homework, but with my head bouncing in rhythm and my eyes glazed over, I become helpless in the grip of a mobile-home commercial, or something by the B-52s. For the past two days my twelve-year-old has been complaining about the Beastie Boys' "Sabotage." It has him in a grip like a snapping turtle.

What evolutionary purpose was served by this mechanism in the brain that grabs something and won't let go? Did humans who had this thing survive better than their neighbors because they had a continuous ditty running through their brains:

"The saber-toothed tiger lives down by the cliff. The saber-toothed tiger lives down by the cliff?" Perhaps their friends whose brains lost track of that information one by one wandered out to the cliff and never came back.

I'm sure things getting stuck in your head was of great value during the years of oral tradition, where one person had to remember the history of the people, while another remembered all the tribe's collective wisdom.

I wish to say something with all due respect to the force in charge of evolution: "We don't need this style of memory now. We have a way to remember important things. It's called WRITING and, I'm trying not to be edgy about this, but we've HAD writing for QUITE A WHILE NOW."

When I am being serenaded by jingle singers, or when the "Gilligan's Island" theme song is on a continuous loop in my head and I'm incapable of thought or coherent conversation, I wonder why the Pentagon bothers with expensive, high-tech weapons. Broadcasting a continuous loop of "It's a Small World After All" would paralyze an invading force from any nation. Soldiers would be staggering in circles, their hands over their ears. They'd be wailing like babies, they'd be begging for release.

When you are helplessly singing the latest Whitney Houston you heard by accident at the mall, what do you do? Most of us, independently from one another, have come up with a solution. I imagine you have as well. The solution? Mind-washing songs. These are the bouncers of the musical world; they will muscle any rowdy thug of a song right out of your brain.

I have conducted a completely unscientific poll, asking people about their most effecting mind-washing song. One friend swears by: "There she was just-a-walking down the street, singing doo-wah-ditty-ditty-dum-ditty-doo." After singing that for two minutes, whatever song has been trying to take over is sent home whining with its tail between its legs. The only drawback is she has "Doo-wah-ditty" stuck in her head for the next day and a half.

A waitress at the Red Lobster uses "Louie, Louie." The guy at the Sandwich Factory swears by Nirvana's "Can't Find a Better Man." My cousin likes the Kinks: "Girl, you really got me now. You got me so I don't know what I'm doing … "

The perfect song-buster is one that banishes the stuck song and then politely leaves without getting itself stuck. The one I use is embarrassing. No one under forty knows it. People mock me for remembering it. This song, though, will chase away doo-wah-ditty. This song will even get rid of the theme song from "Gilligan's Island." It's the one by Tommy Roe that goes, "Dizzy, my head is spinnin'. Like a whirlpool-a it never ends-a, and it's you, girl a-makin' it spin. You're making me dizzy … "

I wonder if I could get a government grant to study mind-paralyzing songs and mind-washing songs. Maybe they would commission a perfect mind-washing song to be written. It would have three chords and a killer hook. It would be scientifically designed to crowd out even the most stubbornly stuck words and melody, then leave politely without residue or aftertaste. I bet the Pentagon would put it in their budget just in case the enemy ever thought of infiltrating our airwaves with a continuous loop of "My bologna has a first name. It's O-S-C-A-R … "

Uh-oh. Now *that* song is stuck in my head. "Dizzy, my head is spinnin' … "

Thoughts about Math

Pat Jobe

I had a thought about math the other day. My wife thought that was a hilarious line.

Between the two of us, my wife and I have lived for a hundred years. You'd think that math would come a little easier after a hundred years. It doesn't.

But here is what I was thinking the other day: Math may be a door to a parallel universe, another world. I ride a lift gate for a living. I push the button and the gate goes up. I push the button and the gate goes down. In and out of the back of my truck I go.

This gives me a lot of time to think about parallel universes and other worlds. I think a lot about the spirit world. I met a man who told me he was dead for twenty-eight minutes one time. He said he talked with his dead father. This is the kind of incident that thrills me and makes my life worth living.

But then it hit me the other day as the lift gate was humming and creaking and I was rising into the air, into the back of my truck. Maybe people don't have to die to enter another world.

Maybe we just have to get better at math. People who are good at math seem to live in another world. They say to me, "Well, I couldn't do it either if I didn't use a calculator," and then they laugh as though the whole issue were the silliest thing. I listen to them talk about the calculator. I know what a calculator is. I probably own three of them, maybe four, and then there's one on the computer. I guess it could be five.

Then I do math in my head, or on a sheet of paper. By math, I mean addition and subtraction. I would never dream of trying long division. But I think I may be onto something. Maybe my reality would change. Maybe I would have more money or need less money or be better with money—if I could just figure out this math thing.

So what about you? How do you get to the next world? What do you find when you get there? How do you get back?

Kevin

Kim Taylor

When my youngest child first asked for a dog, my answer was "no." Plain and simple. She lives in two houses. A dog generally lives in one.

There is already one dog and one cat at this house. At her other house, there is one dog and a varying number of cats.

My youngest child does not accept "no" as an answer.

"I don't want another dog," I told her.

"It will be my dog," she answered.

"He'll have to live at one house," I said.

"Why?" she asked.

After way more discussion than seems reasonable or fun, the moms caved in and agreed she could have a dog. She got dog books from the library and went online to check out breeds of dogs. She settled on a Chihuahua.

This child has the personality of a Lab. She is athletic, adventuresome, and darn near fearless. So when she said Chihuahua, my jaw dropped.

I don't like Chihuahuas. My parents had one when I was very young, and it was not a sweet or pleasant creature. My experiences of that breed have been that they are rarely sweet or pleasant. My friend, Angela, has one she refers to as "the beast." Fortunately, the dog is so old that when she attacks, you are just seriously gummed.

We read about Chihuahuas. The dogs are fiercely loyal, one-person dogs. I knew there would be no dissuading this child. She knows what she wants.

We worked out the details of having another animal among us. The dog would travel with the child, half-time at my house and half with the other mother. Training and care would be the sole responsibility of our youngest child.

And then, out of the blue came the call. A young Chihuahua had been rescued. Angela's daughter found the dog. He had been neglected. They thought he might be a year old. Did we want him?

More discussions. Okay. We'd go take a look at him. Both moms knew that once the child laid eyes on this dog, he'd be coming home with us. And so it was.

Angela had named him Kevin.

"Kevin?"

"Well, he looks like a Kevin," was her response.

"I like it," my daughter smiled.

The first week was pretty rough. There was the whole issue of housebreaking along with the general adjustment period. I don't think Kevin's feet hit the ground much in that first week. He was carried around like a baby most of the time.

And in spite of my feelings about Chihuahuas, Kevin managed to make me like him.

I went to let him out of his kennel one afternoon

for a walk. I opened the door. Kevin came out and immediately rolled over on his back.

I can't help it. I like that in a man.

Fred's Freedom

Meg Barnhouse

It's a freezing morning, and the stray puppy who wandered into the yard with his mama is howling in the dark of our garage. We caught him and put him in a huge crate with food, water, and blankets. We couldn't catch his mama, who is part chow. She is pacing back and forth in front of the closed garage door, a foot of cheap rope hanging from her collar, frayed from where she chewed through it.

The puppy's collar was too tight on its neck, and neither dog had tags. They have a connection with one another, that's obvious. That is why we think the older female is this puppy's mother, although we named her Fred in the first five minutes before we figured that out. She's pacing back and forth, as I said, not with slow deliberate strides, but with running arcs. Her distress is palpable.

I want to find out who owns them. It's not such a good home, that place where they let the puppy's collar get so it was digging into the flesh of his neck, where they tied up the bigger dog with rope. I have taken pictures of the mama, printed them out big and posted them all over. "FOUND," it reads in big letters, then her picture, then my phone number. People have been calling to say they have seen that dog out running their neighborhood for a couple of days, and I needed to come get it. I explain that I FOUND that dog and I'm looking for who owns it.

The child in me wants this to be a Disney movie where the intrepid Fred finds her way home with her puppy. Maybe she finds a better home. The child in me wants to let them go to roam, roam until they find their happy ending. The adult in me knows what the world is like for stray dogs. Our two dogs got loose and traveled five miles from home. Animal Control picked them up, and I was glad.

Here is how the Universe teaches me. I go through what feel like groups of experiences. What I learned from the first one, I'm supposed to use in the next one, connect the dots. I call Animal Control because if I were Fred's owner, that's what I would want me to do. I have a faint hope that they will be claimed. A fainter hope that they will be adopted together. A fair certainty that the puppy will be adopted, but not Fred.

Freedom brings danger. Me? I prefer freedom. Do I have the right to choose that for another being? Before my own dogs got out, I would have been for letting the other dogs just go, find their way, try their luck, be free. Now, I choose safety for Fred and her puppy. Maybe safety will lead to her death. I know I am not the one who controls that. I control so little. I have to do the right thing, the next thing and leave the end of things to luck, to God, to the forces of life. I've got my fingers crossed for Fred. Wish her luck.

Life's Hard

Pat Jobe

Life's hard and then you die. There are a number of variations on that theme. Basically it comes down to that. Life's hard and then you die. If you have ever heard one of these commentaries before, you know I don't believe that. For one thing, I don't believe people die. I've heard too many stories, read too many books, seen too much evidence that human life is eternal, and that what we call death is simply a moving on.

But it's the "Life's hard" part that catches my heart today. I know life is hard. I've had toothaches. You think I'm trying to be funny, but I'm not. One Sunday I was sitting at the table with my sweet Southern Daddy, and I had a toothache. He looked at me and said, "You look like you're hurting pretty bad." I said, "If somebody were doing this to me, I'd have to kill 'em." And I'm a peaceful person.

I've gone through a divorce and cried my heart out over the loss of daily contact with my boys.

Stomachaches, sinus troubles, bad checks, election returns, you name it. Nobody knows the troubles I've seen, but basically I've lived a pretty cushy life. Still I know your life can be much harder; and the lives of people in developing countries, prisons, and cancer wards put us all to shame.

But as Scott Peck says in his *Road Less Traveled*, a book that stayed on *The New York Times* Bestseller List for twenty years, once you accept that life is hard, it gets easier. If I could give you anything right this second, my beloved listeners, it would be that truth, and somehow sink it into your souls.

This all came to light on the morning of October 22. I had spent the day before, October 21, my son Pepper's birthday, wrecking my car, eating too much sugar, going to sleep on the job, and grieving with a member of my church over the death of her sister. Did I mention that I spent an hour and a half with four teenaged girls who like their music loud and change the station every time a commercial comes on?

It was a hard day, the kind of day that makes drug dealers among our wealthiest entrepreneurs, that makes some men think it right to beat their wives, that makes escapism the national religion of America, that makes the La-Z-Boy recliner among our most popular pieces of furniture. But I took no drugs, hit no women (I took a swing at the dog, but she's too fast for me), escaped into no movie about fast cars, bad guys getting blown up, and pretty women getting kissed, and I don't own a Lazy Boy. Instead, I just accepted that it was hard, it was bad, it was nasty, and then I stayed with that for a while.

You think I'm smug and superior about this. I'm not. It stayed pretty bad, pretty hard, pretty nasty well into the night. I wanted to cry. I wanted to moan and groan and complain and pick a fight with God. But, I just stayed with it. Yep, this stinks. This is awful. Yep, not much question about it. This is a pond-scum-sucking situation. Sure enough. Okay. Uh-huh.

The next morning I got up and felt great. I know you hate me now, but it worked. I didn't say I got there through the free and simple practice of deep breathing or through visualizing myself by a mountain stream. I just stayed with the yuk 'til it couldn't yuk me up anymore. It just changes. It has to. Yuk stays yukky when we fight it, kick it, get it drunk or try to have sex with it. When you just let yuk be yuk until it's done, it will get done.

I don't know. I could be wrong. But I think it works. I got it from some Zen article one friend gave me and from a Paul Ferrini book another friend gave me. You just give your whole heart and mind to whatever is going on at the time, and if your life is in the toilet, you don't try to blow up the toilet. Just swim around in the toilet until you can see the way out. It may not work for you, but for me it has been an unyukking miracle.

Cracker Puzzle

Meg Barnhouse

The other day I was sitting at a restaurant with a "country" theme. A rusty sickle hung above my head beside pictures of wholesome-looking white people advertising biscuit flour and lard. While you wait for your food, you can work a puzzle made of a triangular wooden block with plastic golf tees sticking out of holes on one of its sides.

The object of the puzzle is to jump pegs over one another and remove them until only one is left. Painted on the wood are evaluations of your intelligence based on how many pegs you leave on the block. "Leave one, you're genius," it says. "Leave two, you're purty smart. Leave three, you're jes plain dumb. Four or more, *eg-nor-ay-moose.*"

I picked up the puzzle to fiddle with it before breakfast came. Suddenly a picture came to mind. A young man, maybe sixteen, is eating with his family. His Paw thinks he's dumb. Least he says it all the time. All the time laughing at things the boy don't understand, things he ain't learned yet, his Paw treats him like he's the stupidest thang he ever seen. What this boy don't know is that the man that raised his Paw treated *him* like that, and his Paw figgers this is how you treat a son.

The young man picks up the puzzle. He sees his dad notice him pick it up. All the tumblers on the locks in their family patterns start clicking into place. No way to get out of it from here. Best thing would have been to ignore the dern thing but now he has to work it, and if he leaves too many golf tees in place he will hear that chuckle, he will see that look, and something like, " I knowed you was dumb," will scald him again in the same old place. Beads of sweat will gather as he looks the thing over, trying to guess what the tricks to it are, where to start, what to do, and the people at the other tables don't know, can't see the drama being played out here between the boy and his father and his sense of himself, as they both give power to this plastic and wooden toy.

I shake my head to get that story to quit. This is the downside of working as a therapist for twenty years. It's hard to see "normal" any more. You imagine the dramas you've heard about in your office being played out all around you. It takes no effort to do that. What takes effort is blocking out all you know about toxic behavior and allowing for the possibility that most of the folks around you are pretty happy, doing pretty well, thinking about bills and home decor and what to get Dillard and Annie when that baby's born.

I remember when I had heard so much about the abuse people had suffered as children that I would be driving down the street at night, seeing the lights in the windows of the houses, and the thought would come to me: "He's beating them in that house,"

"She's drunk and raging at the kids in that house." I was haunted by images of dark kingdoms, ruled by petty tyrants and cruel dictators, parents fueled by alcohol, fear, and self loathing having free reign with the tender and vulnerable bodies and spirits of the children.

It has taken me some years to heal from the trauma of hearing those stories. I felt like I'd been bitten by snakes. It has taken prayers and deep breathing, acceptance and letting go, rage and writing and learning how to shield myself. There is a shamanic act, a spiritual transmutation that some people learn to do called snake medicine. Where you take venom, take it in without resistance or panic, and, as you heal, your woundedness becomes a healing force for others. All of you who have been snake bit and are transmuting that venom into healing for those around you—now, that's a puzzle worth figuring out.

Single Moms

Pat Jobe

Something happened today I don't ever want to forget. This woman asked her friend, "Is this the guy that wrote the book?" The friend answered yes, then I heard her say to me, "I want to buy it," but that's not really what she said. Instead she said, "I want to borrow it."

An embarrassed moment followed during which the mom said to me, "She's a single mom." It wasn't until later that I realized many of the people who I want to read what I write are people who never buy books because they're single moms.

Single moms are not all poor, but many of them are working their fingers to the bone. Many are shopping in thrift shops and watching for bargains in the grocery store and working second jobs.

They pray and cuss and watch their children sleep the way sailors at sea watch the star-spangled night.

They do without. They wear the same suit they wore last time when the boss throws a dress-up occasion.

They go too long between oil changes and new tires and don't care who sees them alone at the school functions, except when they do.

Single moms waffle between hating their children's fathers for being gone and thanking God Almighty the lousy so-and-so isn't hanging around being a bad influence on the kids.

And when they want to read a book? When they want to shoehorn a few minutes to read in among their endless chores and driving and working and living and dying, they buy one from a used-book store or a yard sale or check it out of the library and pray on their knees they get it back before they have to pay a fine.

And I pray I never forget that single mom.

Revelation

Kim Taylor

The conversation started with the weather. I wasn't eavesdropping so much as overhearing. I was doing paperwork as I waited for my car to be serviced. The minister came over to say hello. We have mutual friends, our daughters have played ball together. We chatted briefly and he left me to my pile of papers.

I heard the other man say something about the Lord always knowing the weather. The minister chuckled and agreed. I shuffled papers. But soon something changed in the tone of the other man. Then I hear him refer to something he'd read in Revelations.

I winced. I'm no Biblical scholar, but I have more minister friends than most people. Both fellow Bubbas are ministers, not to mention my old college roommate.

There is a certain tone people take when they start referring to Revelations.

"No 's,'" Julie, the daughter of a Presbyterian minister, told me.

"What?"

"Just 'Revelation,' no 's' on the end. It is from

the Revelation of Jesus to John."

I told Julie the story of this very sweet Presbyterian minister being lectured to fanatically while we waited for our cars to be serviced. When the minister tried to disagree, the other man told him it was because he needed to read his Bible, or because he hadn't visited this website, or seen this video, or read this book that is eight-by-eleven, over four hundred pages long and costs $64 but was worth every penny.

The pitch, the tone, the cadence of the man's voice intensified as he talked about a secret society that set the currency of the world. How the Vatican had somehow manipulated world power since Woodruff Wilson.

That was the high point for me. Woodruff? I almost laughed with relief. By then I'd put my papers down. I couldn't concentrate. I felt like my ears might begin to bleed. I shifted back and forth in my chair. I had witnessed leaps of logic greater than Evel Knievel would have been able to pull off.

I wondered if the minister had been targeted for this lecture because of his profession. Maybe the man thought he could work magic on a Biblical scholar, make this man of the cloth see the truth. The REAL truth.

All I could see was the door. And then I noticed the minister's wife pull up out front. The minister slapped the other man on the back and told him to have a good day. In what was either divine intervention or just dumb blind luck, my car pulled up. I, too, was saved.

I asked Julie if the book of Revelation is the most misused and misquoted section of the Bible. Julie allowed as how that just might be true. And that it never does seem to be a good thing when people start quoting from it.

Later I wondered what life with this man must look like. Does he lecture about everything? Breakfast, the weather … or does he find a way to make everything about his conspiracy theories.

He said the national debt isn't real. It is created by this secret society. That was where old Woodruff Wilson came in. And where I got out. I got in my newly serviced car and headed for the light.

Possum Babies

Meg Barnhouse

One Sunday I was preaching about depression, and I mentioned that adults who were neglected as children have a high incidence of it. Scientists have experimented on little rat babies, I said, taking them from their little rat mamas for a couple of days at a time, then finding chemicals in their spinal fluid when they grew up that were different from the chemicals in other rats. I just happened to mention that I felt sorry for the little rat babies, having to be experimented on, and then I mentioned that I wished instead that they had done the experiments on little possum babies, since there is a possum family that takes turns waking me up at midnight and then again at 5 a.m., going out and coming into their little apartment they have established under my house. I am mad at all possums these days. They don't care if I sleep well at all.

A few days after I said that, I got an e-mail from a woman in my church who is much kinder and more compassionate than me. She said she wished I would find it in my heart to express more compassion toward the little possum babies. She added that this message wasn't really even from her, it was from her "Mother Nature."

Usually, when I get a note like that I try to search in it for criticism that might be helpful to me, and then shrug the rest off. No, that's a lie. I get mad and defensive first, vow revenge and compose a long letter of self-justification. THEN I calm down, look for what might be useful, erase all the stinky things I wrote and thought, and try to shrug the rest off.

Her letter got me thinking about Mother Nature and the possum babies. The nature-worshippers I know roll their eyes when people tell them what a sweet and nurturing deity the Mother must be, how tender it must be to worship her. Many of them have had actual experience with nature, you know, like outdoors in the winter. In the woods in the summer. Living in a body. Ticks, roaches, frostbite, mosquitoes, cancer.

I decided not to answer this gentle letter of suggestion for my spiritual development, but it was not to be that easy to behave myself. In a crowd at the annual Home Show in town, there she was by a display of wooden shutters.

"Did you get my note?" she asked, sweetly.

"Yes I did, thank you," I said. Not equally sweetly, but almost.

"I just felt it was something you would want to think about," she said. "It wasn't even a message from me, it was from Her."

Okay. I have trouble with people speaking for God. Always have. Whenever someone says they have a message for me from the Spirit, it puts my back up. I don't care whether people call God Him or Her, Allah, Yemayah, or Nana, I have trouble with messages delivered to me through people who want to improve me. If I were more wise, my father used to say, I would love reproof. Maybe I will get there someday.

"The message was from Her?" I asked. "Okay. I have a message for you to give her back from me."

The woman started to protest.

I raised my hand. "Oh, no, please let me finish. If you want to talk about caring for baby possums, you tell Her I care much more than she apparently does, because, even with my feelings about them, I have not killed one. Yet *she*, on the other hand, presides over the deaths of thousands of babies, not only possums, but animals of every kind, at the hands of other animals. And *she* gives no evidence of caring. I mean, you and I could freeze to death in the woods and the breeze would still whisper sweetly in the trees, the moon would still hang silver in the branches, the stars would look on undimmed as our little light went out. When it comes to callousness, I've got NOTHING on Her. I can't hold a candle for her to see by!"

A little part of me was watching and saying, "*Meggie, you are ranting. This woman has taken three steps backward. She does not deserve this.*" But I couldn't stop.

I used to have a friend who would chide me for pulling living pansies out of my garden when they had grown leggy and wild. I should let nature take its course, she said.

Listen, I would tell her. If I were letting nature take its course I wouldn't have planted pansies in the first place! There would be weeds there. I'm a gardener. I pull some things up so the others can go in their place.

I don't fault Mother Nature for having a cavalier attitude toward life and death. A feeling for the sanctity of life is not something for which there is not the slightest smidge of evidence in nature. You have to have death so there is room for life to go on. I don't want it to be mine, or my children's, or my beloved's death, but those will happen eventually. I'm going to keep pulling out pansies when it's their time to go. I don't know when it will be the possums' time to go. If I could just get a good night's sleep, I know I could figure it out.

Dog Food in Heaven

Pat Jobe

Changes are coming. Well, "Duh!" Everything will remain the same. That has a ring of truth to it, too. For the past twelve years, I have lived with my mother-in-law, Patricia Manning. We have talked of baseball and politics. I've brought her library books and one grandson. I have told her more often than I can count that I adore her only daughter, my wife, Pam, the mother of my stepdaughter, Katie, and our son, Luke.

To say we are close would be an exaggeration, but we have had our moments. Once when we were driving together, she suddenly said to me, "You will never know how I appreciate your many kindnesses to me."

Not long ago she moved into Magnolia Manor in Inman, South Carolina. She has since returned home to live with us. But while she was away from us, I was struck by the changes it brought into my life. To live with someone for years and then to suddenly not live with that person brings a quantum shift in reality.

It gave me a little more of Pam's attention, and for you men in radio land who are still in love with your wives, you know how lovely that can be. My home lost its multi-generational charm. My Katie didn't hang out with her grandmother chatting away. Luke didn't head down the hall to show his grandmother something.

But our home was also less demanding. Pam was not waiting on Grandma. I was not waiting on Grandma. There was loss and gain, but behind it all there was the voice of change always coming.

We have had high school graduations—Katie and foster daughter, Sarah, are both in college. Our family will someday be only three, then two, except when the grown kids all come home, then we go back up to nine, except when they bring lovers and friends.

When rocked by change, and this does feel very much like a rocking, I wonder what lasts. When my hourglass holds more sand in the bottom than it does in the top, I wonder if I am just sand.

Oh, I am far too Southern and Protestant not to affirm the land beyond the river that they call the sweet forever, but I keep wondering what I will take with me when I go over there. Will I have fingers and toes? Will I like Key Lime pie? Will there be dogs over yonder? What kind of dog food do they serve in heaven?

Wisdom Tree

Meg Barnhouse

I dragged myself to an early-morning theme talk even though it was the last day of a week at church camp, and I was tired from staying up late singing with friends and dancing my fool head off. A panel of old-timers was talking about the early days of this gathering that now had grown to about a thousand of us coming together every July on the campus of Virginia Tech.

Here is the story that stuck in my mind. There was a teacher who used to come to the camp every summer, a man who could become Thomas Jefferson, Ralph Waldo Emerson, or Theodore Parker. He would bring his class to sit under a large oak tree out on the quad, and the conversation would range over history, philosophy, and theology. Summer after summer, folks would look forward to that class, to sitting under what they came to call "the wisdom tree." They would look forward to having the kind of conversations where you hear and say things that surprise and delight you. One summer night during the church camp, a storm came through. As the people slept, winds and rain whipped the campus. Lightning flashed and struck hard. It struck close. In the morning, daylight revealed the wisdom tree scattered in splinters on the ground.

As the grounds crew came to clear it away, church people came from every corner of the campus to circle round. One by one they asked to take a piece of the tree home with them.

This story struck me deep. I think that there is wisdom available to us, and that it shows up in history, in theology, poetry, music, art, scripture, conversation, nature and ritual. Individuals have a spark of the Divine inside, an inner wisdom that, related to sanely, responsibly, and in community, will lead each person to truth and peace.

Sometimes the place you used to find wisdom gets destroyed. People fail you, a church disappoints you, new information strips away your feeling about a scripture. It's as if your wisdom tree is lying in splinters. We are tempted to take our piece of wisdom home with us and stick it in a place of honor, savoring and celebrating the little piece of wisdom we have, pulling it out whenever there is a new question, a new issue, acting as if that piece of wisdom is self-sustaining, and as if it is enough, on its own, to sustain us.

Acting like this, we are forgetting the crucial next step. What is needed is to bring our piece of the wisdom tree back together with the others and stand together on the roots of our wisdom tree, on the roots of what wisdom we have. We do have it inside us, but it is not enough to hold and savor just the one piece. It needs to be added to the others. You can't walk a good spiritual path all by yourself. You have to be in relationship to a community. Your wisdom needs to have fresh life breathed into it by touching it, again and again to its Source, by bringing it together with the piece of wisdom others carry with them. Then if lightning strikes, if all the places you used to go are ruined, just hold up your piece and we'll find each other.

Beautiful Aliens

Kim Taylor

I used to snicker as my friends debated gender and puberty. I sat smugly as they argued over whether boys or girls were harder to deal with.

Now I am trying desperately to remember every word they said.

I was so glad to get the girls out of diapers and car seats, I never even considered what loomed ahead.

I remember running into the lovely and talented Diane Mance about seven years ago. She had her three children in tow. I had my two little ones. She cooed over them and asked how they were doing. I bragged over Ms. McGillicutie's progress in school, her grades. I carried on about how bright, how quick, how intelligent my children were.

"Ha!" Diane began, one hand on her hip. "Mine used to be smart. But don't worry, they lose it." She pointed to each of her children and reviewed past and present performances. The children stood quietly, obviously having heard this routine before.

I stood with my mouth hanging open. How could this be?

Yesterday, it all flashed back to me.

Ms. McGillicutie was in a cheerful, cooperative mood—a rarity these days as she moves closer to being twelve. I asked her to check the mail as I was headed to the car for something. "Okay," she said brightly and we walked out the front door together.

"There is none," she called. I looked up to see her standing in front of the newspaper box.

I stood like a deer in headlights, swaying and wide-eyed. "Mail! Mail!" I repeated.

"Oh," smiled the beautiful alien creature as she stepped over to the mailbox.

Poor child, her brain is being ravaged by hormones.

I remind myself that Diane's children are now pursuing careers and advanced degrees. That her brilliant offspring were, for a time, beautiful, vacant aliens.

I look at Ms. M and it seems she changes before

my eyes. Sometimes I am visited by the charming and beautiful alien. Sometimes, the Mistress of Hell stays with me.

She asked me if she'd be staying with me or her other mom over the weekend. Me, I told her. "Good," she said, 'cause her other mom has been kind of grumpy.

I think that is called projection.

Her other mom and I like to compare notes. Each of us is hopeful that if the evil one has made a recent appearance, we will be spared. We share conversations we have had with other keepers of aliens. We cling to the stories of the ones who have survived. We remind each other to be strong. It will pass.

I remember grousing over car seats and diapers and being told that was the easy part. It wasn't easy. But it sure was different.

The cuddly, needy, squealing little girls are mostly gone. They have been replaced by creatures so in transition as to be indescribable.

I look at them and wonder what they will become. I am full of hope and fear in a combination that leaves me smiling with a furrowed brow. But I like these creatures. And I look forward to seeing them struggle with car seats and diapers.

Maybe I'm Weak

Pat Jobe

There are actually people in the world who fuss and fight all the time. They rarely ever say a kind word to each other, rarely speak to each other, but when they do, their tone is surly and mean and hurtful.

And these people live together for years. Unlike me, they are not sickened by arguments. They thrive on them, laughing with cackles like the Wicked Witch in *The Wizard of Oz*, who promises to "Get you, my pretty, and your little dog, too." It takes a mean person to want to get a dog, too.

This strikes me because I am painfully aware of my addiction to peace in the family. I hate fights, though I cause as many as the rest of my family members combined. Our family has been under a lot of stress here lately. Things that were already pretty bad have gotten worse.

Although I warned myself that these are the kinds of situations that take my normally sunshiny personality and make it snappy, my self did not heed the warning. My self rose up like a viper and snapped something surly and smart alecky; and as I write these words, I am languishing in the frosty silence of my wife Pam's anger.

Just a few days before, I did it again. Apparently I do it about every third or fourth day. One such incident dragged a curse from my wife's innards and made her swear, "I don't know why I married you," which prompted my stepdaughter, Katie, to pipe, "I've wondered that the whole time."

I recently groveled and begged to be placed back in Pam's good graces when she said, "You hate for anybody to be mad at you." I knew it was true. Just hours before, I had answered a wrong number; and the woman became irate with me because I was not the person she had called. When I told her I needed to catch another line, she fumed, "I didn't want to talk to you anyway. You sound like a very unsuccessful and untalented bum."

I was pretty sure she was right and spent the next good while wallowing in self-pity. But there are people who talk like that all the time, who especially talk to their own families with rudeness, vitriolic jabber, and verbal brickbats. Such folks are perfectly happy to make each other miserable¯and that, dear Bubbas, is quite a revelation to me.

It makes me feel strange and weird and insipid, as if my need for peace and goodwill is a weakness, and perhaps I would do better if I cackled like a witch and threatened to get everyone around me¯and their little dogs, too.

Money

Kim Taylor

I've spent all morning waltzing with my fear of money and my vacuum cleaner. I vacuumed and thought. Then I wrote about my thoughts. I called Meg Barnhouse and read to her.

"Mmmm," she said.

"Okay. What is wrong with it?" I ask.

"Oh, there is nothing wrong with it. It's just sort of … well … bland."

"Why?"

"Because you didn't talk about what you are afraid of," Meg says gently.

"That's because my fears are stupid."

Laughter comes through the phone as Meg says, "Perfect."

I was so glad I called.

I had worked so hard to face my fears by not actually looking at them. And it might be embarrassing to talk about them.

Most of us are afraid of money. Why is that?

Well, my fears about money tie directly to my fears of being stupid. If I don't handle my money well, use it wisely, it will prove once and for all that I'm an idiot. I'll be homeless, or worse yet, living in the spare room of my mother's trailer.

Too much of this fear has to do with how other people see me.

Am I successful?

Geez, what does that mean?

It reminds me of my children asking if we were rich. I remember my parents' answer to that question. Well, I remember my mother saying "no" and my dad's answer being too long to follow. What my grandmother said was that we were very rich because we had each other.

But that is not what my children want to know. They want to know how we measure up.

This is the bottom line. How worthy are we—all measured in dollars and cents?

But I'm not quite that cynical.

I tell my children that we have everything we need and most things we want. That is not as much as some people and lots more than others have.

That satisfies them.

I wish it satisfied me.

I am afraid of money. I'm almost as afraid of having money as I am of not having money.

I think the dangers of having money and using it poorly—stupidly, losing it or throwing it away—are as great as the dangers of having no money.

So I am presently telling myself I have just the right amount of money. I have everything I need and most things I want.

But the truth is I'd like to trust myself enough to risk having money. Enough money to do something stupid and enough sense to do something wonderful.

Wish You Were Here

Meg Barnhouse

Once in a while, in this life, you catch a glimpse of what it's supposed to be like.

We were having our monthly music jam, and the regulars were there. Doug plays fiddle, and his teenage son, Owen, brought his electric guitar. Owen was in his Marilyn Manson T-shirt. It's usually that, or Bowie. Ed, who is my age, late forties, plays mandolin. Other folks had guitars and drums, and some came to sing the harmonies. We take turns starting a song, and the others join in as it goes. Most of the folks my age were playing folk music. No cheesy songs about froggies, no Kumbaya. I tried to outlaw John Denver, but you have to pick your battles. We had played John Hiatt, Emmylou Harris, some Rolling Stones, Indigo Girls, Appalachian sex and death songs, a couple of old gospel things.

We had just finished "Angel Band," and it was Owen's turn. Head down, he fingered the strings while we waited to see what he would want to play. I don't know if he was feeling shy, or if his energy had been sapped by too much folk music. His dad said "Come on, Owen, play that Pink Floyd thing you were working on." Owen's fingers found the opening riff to "Wish You Were Here." Then he sighed, and all the wind seemed to go out of his sails. He muttered, "Naw, I pass, I guess."

"Don't do that," Ed said, and started to pick out the notes on his mandolin. Owen's dad picked up the notes on the fiddle. Owen's head came up, and he started the chords. We tried to figure out when to jump in. "So, so you think you can tell …" We had come in at the wrong place. Owen started nodding his head to show us the beat. He said, "NOW," and we began again. " … heaven from hell? Blue skies from pain? … " By the end of the song we were all grinning like fools. Yeah. Yeah. Pink Floyd on the fiddle, mandolin, and electric guitar, a sixteen-year-old and a forty-six-year-old playing a song about a feeling everyone has sometimes. That's what I'm talking about. Wish you'd been there.

Which Number?

Pat Jobe

My seven-year-old son, Luke, created a construction-paper heart with a number sign on it. I'm sure that was not his intention. Surely he just meant the intersecting blue strips of paper as texturing for his pink paper heart; but there it is, a number sign as clear as the morning dew.

My question came instantly. Which number? He is most reluctant to marry or even practice serious courtship, which at seven, I think, is good.

So I think he is not interested in the number two, no coupling for him, no being paired to a partridge in a tree.

Three is a good number. He asks me if it's a lucky number; and I tell him it is one of the luckiest. I know it's good for a heart number, because he and his mother and I make a musketeer-like trio. Most definitely we are one for all and all for one. What a world it would be if that motto could be made universal.

Four conjures the winds: North, South, East, and West. There are four bases in that ballgame he likes. Four balls and take your base. He likes the Fourth of July.

Try five. With his two teenage sisters that makes a family outing. He claims to have once played until five in the morning.

The list could go on and on, but there is a number I think you'll never find listed in Luke's heart. I could be wrong, but he rarely strives to be number one. He wants his way but yields easily when the battle goes to others. He is a friend, a team player, not a loner, not a solitary man. He would make a lousy Lone Ranger, unless he found a fine Tonto. He is a great partner, plays well with others.

Maybe this is wishful thinking on my part. Maybe I have done too much yielding in my life, not fought hard enough to be number one. Still I like team players; and as I look at his paper heart, my prayer is that his real heart will always be full of numbers higher than one.

Manners & Mean People

Kim Taylor

Today, I learned why I don't have magic powers or carry a handgun.

At the drive-through window at the bank, I got in line behind a truck. Within seconds, I was angry. In the center of the back window of the truck was a Confederate flag. I'm sort of used to seeing them. I don't like it. But I accept that to some it is an acceptable emblem of the South. Beside the flag, there was one of those Calvin (of Calvin and Hobbes) decals. You know, the ones that show the cartoon character urinating on some other make of automobile. Well, this Calvin was urinating on the word "everybody." This little symbol of community caused my teeth to grind.

I wouldn't have been happy to see the flag. I was amused by the other decal that read "proud to be a redneck." But the piss-on-everybody statement from a teenaged white boy caused my blood to boil.

I wanted to go find his parents and smack them.

Here's an attitude the world needs more of.

It reminded me of what my friend Allison

Costello had said years ago: "Litter is a redneck's political statement."

And as I sat growing older and more irritable, I realized that this young punk had not prepared anything for his trip through the drive-through window. He did not care one whit that traffic was lining up behind him. He didn't have a pen. He even had to have a long conversation with the teller after he got his envelope.

Then he pulled away from the window and stopped. I had just enough room to pull up to the window. But I only had to cash a check. I was done in seconds. And stuck.

I tapped my horn.

I REALLY wanted to drag him out of the truck and give him a stern lecture about what an inconsiderate little snot he is. I wanted to stand on my horn. I wanted to tap his bumper with mine, pushing him out of my way. But I really did just tap the horn.

He wheeled around, sticking his head out of the window as if I had tapped his bumper with mine. "Got a problem?" he asked.

"You!" I yelled back.

I am not proud of my behavior. I was shaking with rage. Guys like that believe themselves to be entitled.

I know therapists, theologians, and really nice people would say that people like this boy really are afraid. And they are puffing out their chests to keep anyone from getting too close.

They are rude, crude and need to be taught how to behave in public. Not to mention at home alone with their alleged loved ones.

These are mean people. As the bumper sticker says, "Mean people suck."

And they make me mean.

If nice people didn't just let them be mean with no consequences, they'd quit. But they are bullies. They keep being bullies because it gets them what they want. We don't teach them any differently.

The bank teller didn't say, "Excuse me, sir, but you'll have to come in to complete this transaction."

I think it's about drawing lines. They don't have to be laws. Not rigid or unbending. But treating the people in the world around you like human beings is not a trait you are born with. It is something you have to be taught.

I'm trying to teach my kids manners. They are as resistant as I was as a kid. It isn't too much trouble. It doesn't make them weak. You can be nice without being a doormat. And you can say no to mean people.

This rude kid made me mad. I didn't teach him anything. I didn't get through to him.

But he got through to me.

Dr. Max

Meg Barnhouse

I'm playing Dr. Max on the computer, matching colored pills to each other end to end as they fall faster and faster. I have been doing this since an old man I loved died a couple of months ago. The sound of the game is turned off because I have the TV on the E! Entertainment Channel. I'm watching the *True Hollywood Story of Corey Feldman*. The former child actor was obsessed with Michael Jackson. He'd learned all his dance moves, dressed like him and everything. He had trouble with his father cheating him out of money.

Those parental managers sometimes break bad that way. Drugs claimed him, but he was finally clean. Of course, he had lied about being finally clean some years ago while doing anti-drug commercials and shooting up. This time he says he is telling the truth. I snort cynically and fit another pill into its place.

I love the *True Hollywood Story*. The spotlight of fame burns too brightly and the star flames out. Alcohol, usually, or drugs. You get to see what people look like now. You wonder how they can look so good with all they've been through. You get to see their friends and former colleagues talk about them. People shake their heads and say fame is hard to handle. They say getting so much money makes life complicated. I can imagine. The moral of many of these episodes seems to be that money can't buy happiness. I think sometimes it would buy happiness, if you just could stay sober. I guess some people just need some oblivion now and then. They can't take the feelings of real life. It's too much for them … HA I broke five rows. Big points add up in the corner of my computer screen. What was I talking about? Oh, yeah. Oblivion. Yep, I guess some people just need it more than others.

There is that pressure to produce and to look great all the time. I know that would make me nuts. You'd have to stay so thin. I can't even stay a little bit thin. Maybe that's where the drugs come in. I briefly wonder what kind of drugs I would have to do to be thin, and what effect that would have on my health overall. I think about my children, having to live with a drugged-out mother. She would be unavailable. Of course, I have been a little bit unavailable here with my back to them, playing Dr. Max. Oh, there goes another row. They are about to be going too fast for me. I've beat this level before, though. I can do it. If not this game, then the next one. And I did burn the dinner last night because I was trying to play Dr. Max while it was cooking. When I'm looking at the screen and the pretty colors, everything else goes away. I don't think about anything but that, and that doesn't take too much thought. It's like my brain becomes one of those pinpoint dots, like those laser pointers.

Yeah, I'm glad my children have a mother who

doesn't feel a need for oblivion. And who is not addicted to anything. Oh, man! I can beat that score. One more game.

The Joy of Writing

Pat Jobe

My fourth-grade writing teacher planted a seed of encouragement. "Pat Jobe is a writer," she said to a roomful of nine- and ten-year-olds, most of whom cared little. But I cared.

She suggested my parents buy me a typewriter. They did.

My buddy, a dear friend since high school, said, "I love it when you write with abandon."

Like a drunk in the street after our team won the state championship or the Rose Bowl or the heart of a girl I'd been watching from afar, that's the kind of writing my teacher and my buddy both like.

And who can argue? Writers like to be liked. But deeper than the feedback is the spark that strikes dry kindling when we actually do the writing, sit in front of a screen or a blank sheet of paper; and those lovely little scratches start lining up. Save a child from drowning? Listen to a first-grader sing? Fight for a good cause? Win an election? Make love? It can be done in the most minute detail or painted with the broadest stroke by writing about it.

Yeah, right, the cynic objects. Writing the thing, describing it on paper, is not the thing itself. Don't tell it to a girl to whom I wrote a love note in college. She said I went too far. The record needs to show it's also as far as I got.

Kurt Vonnegut said he could do nothing about the chaos around him, but he could reduce to perfect order the words on an eight-and-a-half-by-eleven sheet of paper. Add to that, it is an immense pleasure.

Smoke between old friends by a fire, whispers of love in the dark, tips of fingers against familiar skin, strong drink, answered prayer, sunsets, a photograph of a marsh where one friend saw the three-year-old sprint and mused, "I love to watch that boy run," a candle by the bedside, the list is fodder for a dozen novels or notes stuffed in envelopes, dispatched on email.

Yes, there are also politics and spirit and business transacted on paper. Scrawled and hammered lines have moved armies, hearts, and fortunes. Says who? By God, I've got it in writing.

But the people who do it for fun may be the most dangerous alive. Tom Robbins talks about being insane by design. It is like that. Jack Kerouac remembers those with jingle-jangle energy who never sigh or say a commonplace thing. It is most certainly like that.

After 30 years of newspaper columns and radio

commentaries, one novel, and a collection of essays, the best lines are the "ah-ha's" where readers find themselves, their children, their dreams, their aces in the hole. But who cares? The best lines for me are the ones where I find myself or better yet, lose myself.

The strangest thing is to create a world on paper and for a few minutes or a few hours, live there. Readers like that, too.

Loss

Kim Taylor

I watched the nearly-full moon set over the mountains. She went down just as the orange of the sun replaced her white glow.

Soon I will shower and change. I will make my way to the funeral Mass being held for Tony Lynch. I will sit with friends I have known for twenty-five years. I will cry.

Then I will hug my friends good-bye and return to my house not a mile away. My children will be here cleaning and arguing and laughing. Around noon, my new love will arrive. We will have lunch, the four of us. We will talk about the death of my youngest child's dog the day before.

But now, while the house is quiet, while the children are sleeping and the sun is rising, I sit alone with my coffee and I lament the passage of time.

Maybe it is because I will turn fifty this year. The oldest child will take driver's ed. My youngest child will become a teenager. And I will grow closer to this woman I've been waiting for all my life. Maybe it was that Tony was only fifty-one with three children, two of whom were younger than my own.

I've heard this happens to people my age¯that one morning we wake up and realize there are more miles behind us than ahead of us. We've spent all our lives at breakneck speed trying to get to this very place. Now we see it all rushing past as the train speeds on.

I wouldn't change anything. Well, maybe a few things. But I know that it took all those nanoseconds to make this one. And I wouldn't change this one for all the world.

All the clichés I've ever heard are rushing at me like a stampeding herd. I sit at my computer laughing at them all. There is nothing new to say about this place. Nothing I can say that will tell my children that each minute is a gift, a prize to cherish.

My youngest child cried herself to sleep last night surrounded by dog toys, the carrier, the blanket and collar. I kissed her cheek and told her to dream of the good times. I also told her she would hurt for a while. She is supposed to hurt for a while. Slowly that hurt will pass, but for now her big old heart is full of sadness. She nodded. I turned out the light.

Today she will wake to sadness—not to the

squirming creature who would lick her out of sleep.

I will try to explain to her that learning to grieve is something most of us are really bad at. We don't want to feel pain. We want to make it go away. I would like to make hers go away. But it is important for her to feel this loss. She must still get up and take care of her life, and she must take care of her life with this pain in her heart.

I have had coffee with this odd couple of pain and joy. I think I'm only just beginning to understand how much room there is in my heart. I feel the blessing of the full moon and the rising sun. The joy of my family and the loss of my friend.

This quiet moment, the train seems to have slowed just a bit.

I Won't Give Up

Pat Jobe

Okay, I'll admit it. I've ruined my life. I've given up a third of my income, I live away from my family at least three nights a week, and I bought a business two hundred miles from home that requires hundreds of hours of solitude and manual labor, and which may or may not get me any closer to living my dream life.

It's awfully tempting to abandon all my dreams and lie about ever having any in the first place.

Sometimes I imagine my funeral and the people who know me and love me best shaking their heads and saying, "What a great guy. He came so close. Wonder why he never made the big time."

But I won't give up because there is another group who have always thought I was insane or a deluded egotist or some other type of pitiful loser, and those are the ones I have to keep dreaming against.

They won't be surprised if I never make *The New York Times* Bestseller List or sell a song to a major entertainer or get out of debt.

The first girl I dated called me crazy the whole time and wonders to this day how I roam freely. One of my employees in a candy store I managed said terrible things about my mother and questioned my intelligence. Even my friends have sometimes attacked me so hard as to make me recoil and shudder.

I can't give up my dreams and prove all my detractors right.

So I sit in the parking lot of the Dollar General Store in Ladson, South Carolina, so grateful for all my supporters and so determined to show up all those who think me a cornball lunatic.

As I sit here writing, two young men walk by grinning with their shirttails hanging out.

I want to shout to them, "Live your dreams! Have a wonderful life! Never give up! Reach for the stars! Tuck in your shirttails."

Timber!

Meg Barnhouse

I don't know if you believe in omens. I do, in a casual way though, not on the lookout for meaningful flocks of geese in the sky or cows gazing at me in a significant manner.

I was curious to know, though, what the following events might portend. You know how, at a certain stage of a new love, you go meet the person's family, you spend time talking about what commitment might mean to you, you feel the other person out about how much they love you versus how much you love them, you wonder together about what the future holds for you as a couple. Anyway, we had just been with my new beloved's whole family, up near South Mountain State Park in North Carolina. We decided, just the two of us, to ride up to the park, talking as we went.

By the time we got to the park, the conversation was at That Point. The place where the other person has revealed how they feel and now it's your turn, and they want to know how you feel, and what commitment means to you and whether you might want to do it. And I did. I did want to do it, but I didn't want to talk about it yet.

We had parked by a creek and, still talking, had walked to the broad wooden bridge that crossed the creek. There was a large Pakistani family enjoying a picnic, about thirteen of them chatting and walking back and forth between the bridge and their vans, saris fluttering in the breeze like exotic flowers. We stood on the bridge, looking down into the water, which was way down because there had been a drought. I was thinking about commitment and family, my arms folded across my chest, apparently backing away from my beautiful friend as I fumbled for words to express my hopes, my fears.

We heard a sharp crack like the sound of a gun being fired. It came from up the hill in the woods. More cracking sounds followed, like that sound in the movies when a tree is falling. Oh! It was a tree. An enormous tall oak tree whose top was now tilting toward us, not tilting really, falling. Yep, only lots faster than trees fall in the movies, and straight at us on the bridge. Intelligent Pakistanis scattered while I was musing about how they must slow down the film when they show a tree falling in movies, and I never thought of that before. I started thinking about what else they slowed down in movies, and thought probably they slowed the fights down, so all those moves I thought I might remember to make from my karate classes most likely wouldn't even stir inside my head until I was lying in a pile of broken bones on the sidewalk.

Surely that tree wasn't going to reach the bridge, but by gum it was starting to look as if it might reach us for real. What to do? Well, sometimes when a tornado comes and you are out in the open, you are supposed to lie down, and this felt on about the same order as a tornado. I started to lie down and cover my head so I would get injured only the minimum amount. I heard a voice shouting, "NO," and I felt my beloved pulling on my hand. I stumbled a little, because I was almost kneeling by that time, but I took four or five steps and turned around in time for the topmost branch of the gigantic oak to tear a little gash in my elbow.

Fortunately my beloved knew, after eight years in the army and lots of practical living, that they slowed down the film when they showed trees falling in the movies, and trained reactions kicked in. I was pulled to safety. We stood there looking at where we had been standing, at the bridge now completely covered by this huge fallen tree.

What am I supposed to make of that, other than that I should not ruminate about the movies until I get out of the way of falling trees? Did my friend save my life? What did it mean that a tree fell on us while we were talking about our future? My friends at the coffee shop decided it meant that the enormous, rigid ideas I had about commitment were falling over, and they might have killed me except for this relationship pulling me to safety. Yeah, that's got some life in it for me. I'll stick with that.

Politics

Kim Taylor

So, is it just me, or does it seem the height of irony that little more than two months after another very questionable election here at home, our government is off around the globe monitoring elections in other countries? Is it to see if the elections are held fairly or is it to make sure things come out the way "we" want?

I am still reeling from months of political advertising that kept me slack-jawed. Just when I thought family values might be laid to rest, here it comes in a new dress: the sanctity of marriage between a man and a woman.

Holy cross-dressing, Batman.

Not that long ago, it was God, Country, and Family Values. I can still remember, "America, love it or leave it." Now it is "Support our Troops," as if wanting them to come home safe and all in one piece is not supportive.

It is the same message, boys and girls, same song, second verse …

I want us to recognize the tune. The fear-mongers are singing. Listen carefully.

Less than one month after the election, more than half the country believes the war in the Middle East is not justifiable. Hello, did you people vote?

Hi, over here … yes, it's me again. Still working.

Still paying my taxes. Still raising children. Active in my community and my church. Still voting. And still getting it wrong.

I'm not giving up. I'm going to keep living my life right in front of you. Right next door. Right across the street. Right in line at the grocery store. On bleachers at basketball games. In the carpool lane at school.

I'm here plugging away just like the rest of you. Trying to make ends meet. Wondering if I'm doing an okay job as a parent. Wondering if Social Security will exist by the time I get there.

Me with the two children I didn't birth and the female partner. Yep, me, the liberal.

Carrying On

Pat Jobe

If I really am among the most optimistic people some of my friends know, the world is truly grim. And if the world is truly grim, if millions and millions of people are dragging themselves from day to day despite horrible waves of depression, fear, bad moods, crankiness, and despair, then human life on this planet is even more of a miracle than I thought it was.

If most married people really do just barely tolerate each other, then the amazing fact is not that so many kill each other, but rather that so few do. If work is all that boring and tedious, we should take note that such a tiny percentage of people abuse drugs and alcohol, have affairs, kill their bosses, and commit suicide.

I thought for years that most people have decent marriages, raise nice kids and don't kick their dogs. Now it occurs to me that maybe I'm wrong about that, and yet people don't run madly in the streets screaming and tearing their hair.

War, disease, famine, genocide, and reality television march along like regular visits from the guy who sprays for bugs, and yet people still make it to work and school, the grocery store, the movies, church, and the playground.

There's an old bumper sticker that reads, "If you aren't outraged, you aren't paying attention." Well maybe that's wrong. Maybe millions of people are paying attention, and they just don't see much future in being outraged.

They are carrying on. And for some cussed reason, that gives me hope.

Everything Must Change

Meg Barnhouse

Everything must change. Nothing stays the same … Judy Collins sang it on my stereo in college. She gave it such a melancholy sound. In moving into a new house, I was going though a pile of papers. There was a $20 gift certificate from a couple who aren't together anymore to a restaurant that is not there anymore. Pity about the restaurant. Harry's on Morgan Square was a good one, high ceilings, good food, walls painted deep teal, early nineties style. Am I sad about the restaurant? A little. As a minister I deal with the oceans of suffering just under the surface in many people. I have more immediate things to feel sad about.

Still, I had a moment of sadness, coming across the certificate. It was a waste, my not having used the gift. Did I just lose it, or was I waiting until just the right occasion, an occasion that never arrived? Was it a waste for the folks to have opened an elegant restaurant that didn't last forever? No. Harry's is part of the history of this town. Now, ten years later, people still say, "It's right down the sidewalk from—remember where Harry's used to be? It's right down from there." That room is part of the memories of countless couples who had anniversaries there, people who had job interviews there, people who fell in love there.

Am I sad about the couple? They seemed well-matched, both nice looking, funny and smart. They had a divorce that was fairly amicable, as divorces go. Was it a waste for them to have been together, since the marriage didn't last until death? Not at all. Their two daughters are grown into good people. One of them just got married herself. The creation of those human beings made it worthwhile, along with the happy times they had, the things they learned from one another, the life they made. Just because a relationship doesn't last until you die doesn't mean it was not meant to be, that it wasn't true and real.

Everything must change. We know that. We wouldn't want everything to stay just the same. Lots of times things change for the better. Sometimes they change for the worse. Lots of times they just change for the different. Why do I feel sad at the changes, if I know that's true? You know what? I don't need a reason to feel sad. It just comes, and then it goes. Who said every feeling needs a reason? Change is satisfying and it's melancholy, and it can be both at the same time.

It was kind of that couple to give me money for a nice dinner. I see by the date on the certificate that they gave it to me on my first birthday after I'd ended my marriage. I was still living in an apartment with only the bare necessities for my children and me. I had a new job I loved, and I loved my new life. Making those changes was the hardest thing I've ever done. It was hard on everyone involved, but the change was life-giving for me. Sad? Yes. Satisfying? Definitely. Nothing stays the same. I can live with that.

There You Go

Pat Jobe

A phrase has been working its way into my speech lately. I like it a lot. Although I recognize a certain danger in repetitive phrases, this one has power.

It's "There you go."

I say it most when people are saying something is a certain way, but also it is another way. Case in point: Two married friends of mine are driving each other crazy. He says she is manipulative, gamey, coy, a spendthrift and a cheat. Then he says he loves her, adores her, can't live without her. To which I say, "There you go."

It seems to satisfy people, although I'll be dipped in dog doobers if I can figure why. People don't really care what I say back, especially when telling me their troubles, so all I really need to do is make noises that say, "I'm listening."

Other folks will say, "I hear ya'," or "Yeah," or "Of course." But I'm just crazy about "There you go." It hands all the power back to the person who has all the power. It's as though their words and my response are both enormously powerful and mysterious. My friend with the less-than-but-so-much-more-than-desirable wife is the only person who can deal with his feelings. He asks me what I think he should do. I tell him, and he tells me he's already tried that. I know for a fact that he has not, but there you go. It's his boat to row, his row to hoe, and his hole card to show.

It sets me free. Like a diagnosis of nothing's wrong with you, like a judge dismissing the charges, like my baby saying it's party time, this tiny ten-letter phrase relieves me of solving other people's problems (mine are baffling aplenty), carrying other people's loads (my feet hurt thinking of my own), and saving the world (although I still kinda cling to that one).

My ex-wife asked me the other night on the phone if I had finally given up on saving the world. Well, kinda. You see, I'm Woodstock vintage. Two hundred thousand people listening to Joan Baez just did something for me. No, I wasn't actually there, but I saw the movie, and wished so badly I had been there, especially for Joan Baez. Twenty-five years later, she played Sarajevo during the worst of that city's war and told about Serbian shelling setting a Bosnian apartment house on fire, and how she saw the Bosnian Muslims huddle in the cold and watch their apartment house burn, how suddenly the local volunteer fire department, comprised entirely of Serbian Christians, came and put out the fire. Yes, it's sad and absurd and crazy, but is also hopeful in a sort of Marx

Brothers way.

I believe the word is healing itself, although there's still lots to be done. You probably think I'm crazy. You may well think all the evidence of good is just statistical anomaly and that evil really is in charge, running roughshod over every Cinderella who ever wished upon a star. Well, there you go.

Crab Apples & Granny Ruth

Kim Taylor

I've been picking up crab apples. I'm about to be part of some magic. I have raked and picked and discarded crab apples for two straight days.

The weather is cool. The wind from the far rim of the hurricane clears the air, giving me an energy that only autumn provides. I sit on a piece of cardboard and pick through the marble-sized apples. Mottled red and yellow, they are beautiful piled in my basket.

I pick them for my Granny Ruth.

She is not my granny, but she is the closest thing to a maternal figure I have in my life. She is a grandmother to my children. She is much more than that to me.

I think she doesn't know how much I love her.

I am picking the crab apples for her.

I think I am not so good at love. I don't seem to

show it the way the people around me expect.

I keep so many people I love in my heart. They are constantly in my thoughts. But the days seem so short and pass so quickly. It can be months, even years before I make contact.

Granny Ruth gets me in spurts. I will spend hours with her, bringing in loads of crab apples. Catching up.

I think about this as I choose the best apples from the ground.

I also think about my connections to my family of origin. I am tired of being a disappointment to them.

I think about Granny Ruth. I may disappoint her at times. But it never seems to interfere with her love for me. She fusses and it is like being hugged.

We are worlds apart. But we find places to be together.

Sometimes my hurts remind her of her own. She has had many hurts in her eighty-some years. We sit quietly. Neither of us wanting to cry.

Then she will tell me some tale of Uncle Jay and we will laugh again. I will tell her some story of Scooter, and she will throw back her head and laugh from her heart.

I sort out the best crab apples. Knowing she will sort them again. She will stand at her kitchen sink, washing and sorting. She will chat and sort and chuckle. "Now, Kimberly," she will chide me for bringing her rotten apples. She will tease me about tracking dirt in her house or not washing the dishes I have dirtied while there.

Things happen in that kitchen. Making and mending. I think she must know more about magic and healing than anyone I know. I can hear her say, "Now, Kimberly."

I am not the only one who calls her Granny Ruth. Though she lives alone in her house, it is rarely empty. Her family is a varied collection of souls who have wandered through her kitchen and have not been able to stay away.

A glass of tea. A piece of pie. The laugh that comes from her heart. These are the offerings of her kitchen. And we line up to dine.

I am bringing crab apples. They are tiny and sour.

Granny Ruth will make them into treats that will be ours for the asking. She will hand out the jars of jelly and tell tales of how "that Kim Taylor brought these to me."

And for a little while, I will be part of the magic.

Meet the Bubbas

Meg Barnhouse grew up in North Carolina and Philadelphia and now makes her home in Spartanburg. She travels nationwide as a speaker, singer/songwriter and humorist has also been heard on National Public Radio's "Weekend All Things Considered." Meg is the mother of two wise, funny and handsome sons, ages 14 and 17. She has a second-degree black belt in karate, has published two other books, *Waking Up the Karma Fairy* and *Rock of Ages at the Taj Mahal*, and has recorded a CD, *July Blue*, a mix of original songs and stories. To buy her other merchandise, visit ***www.megbarnhouse.com***.

Pat Jobe is a former preacher, newspaper man, and frozen meat salesman who now drives a 24-foot rag truck. His friend Meg Barnhouse once heard him say, "I'm a truck-driving novelist," to which she said, "That'll work on a book jacket." His one novel, *365 Ways To Criticize The Preacher*, is in its second printing. His column runs in nine weekly newspapers. Radio Free Bubba is heard Wednesday mornings on WNCW, 88.7, and occasionally on "Your Day," the noon show from South Carolina's ETV Radio. He has lived with eight children, four of whom came to his family through the foster care system. Only Luke is still living at home with Mama Pam, Grandmama Patsy, five dogs, and one cat. His email address is *patjobe@chesnet.com*.

The ever-reluctant writer, ***Kim Taylor*** avoids writing by remodeling a post-Victorian house she and her partner, Deb, purchased in the summer of 2004. They share the house with the now teen-aged Scooter (Jai) and Ms. McGillicutie (Tori); cats, Dewayne and Chiro; and the bad dog, Belle.

The Hub City Writers Project serves readers and writers by publishing works that foster a sense of place and by sponsoring events and programs. Our metaphor of organization purposely looks backward to the nineteenth century when Spartanburg was known as the "hub city," a place where railroads converged and departed. As we enter the twenty-first century, Spartanburg has become a literary hub of South Carolina with an active and nationally celebrated core group of poets, fiction writers, and essayists. We celebrate these writers—and the ones not yet discovered—as one of our community's greatest assets. William R. Ferris, former director of the Center for the Study of Southern Cultures, says of the emerging South, "Our culture is our greatest resource. We can shape an economic base...And it won't be an investment that will disappear."

—Hub City Titles—

- *Hub City Anthology* • John Lane & Betsy Teter, editors
- *Hub City Music Makers* • Peter Cooper
- *Hub City Christmas* • John Lane & Betsy Wakefield Teter, editors
- *New Southern Harmonies* • Rosa Shand, Scott Gould, Deno Trakas, George Singleton
- *The Best of Radio Free Bubba* • Meg Barnhouse, Pat Jobe, Kim Taylor, Gary Phillips
- *Family Trees: The Peach Culture of the Piedmont* • Mike Corbin
- *Seeing Spartanburg: A History in Images* • Philip Racine
- *The Seasons of Harold Hatcher* • Mike Hembree
- *The Lawson's Fork: Headwaters to Confluence* • David Taylor, Gary Henderson
- *Hub City Anthology 2* • Betsy Wakefield Teter, editor
- *Inheritance* • Janette Turner Hospital, editor
- *In Morgan's Shadow* • A Hub City Murder Mystery
- *Eureka Mill* • Ron Rash
- *The Place I Live* • The Children of Spartanburg County
- *Textile Town* • The Hub City Writers Project
- *Come to the Cow Pens!* • Christine Swager
- *Noticing Eden* • Marjory Heath Wentworth
- *Noble Trees of the South Carolina Upstate* • Mark Dennis, John Lane, Mark Olencki
- *Literary South Carolina* • Edwin Epps
- *Magical Places* • Marion Peter Holt
- *When the Soldiers Came to Town* • Susan Turpin, Carolyn Creal, Ron Crawley, James Crocker
- *Twenty* • Kwame Dawes, editor

colophon

The Return of Radio Free Bubba was re-recorded with another new look for 2005. The 5 x 7 format was digitally engineered using the lastest...***yada, yada, yada...bah, bah, bah... techno stuffies and thingies*** that every graphic guy and gal now uses to perfect high-quality books such as the one you are now holding. No animal testing was used on the final manuscript production. However, much chocolate, in various forms and flavors, was consumed to keep the creative juices flowing.